To Barbara

Enjoy the journey.

Every Success

LEADERSHIP LAID BARE

THE NAKED TRUTH OF GREAT LEADERSHIP

GRAHAM WILSON Leadership Expert and Author

Founder of Successfactory™

HOW TO BECOME A SUCCESSFUL LEADER IN TODAY'S WORLD

PART OF THE LEADERSHIP LAID BARE SERIES   **#LEADERSHIPREVOLUTION**

First paperback edition printed 2015 in the United Kingdom
Reprinted with revisions 2015, 2018

A catalogue record for this book is available from the British Library.

ISBN 978-0-9931390-0-0

Published by Success Online, Chester, United Kingdom
For more copies of this book, please email: info@thesuccessfactory.co.uk
Tel: +44 (0) 1829 771770

Printed in Great Britain

Illustrations by Martin Teviotdale

Printed on sustainable paper

"LET'S START A LEADERSHIP REVOLUTION."

GRAHAM WILSON

Meet the Author

A personal message from Graham

Welcome to Leadership Laid Bare. Over the past 21 years I have had tremendous success developing many great leaders. It is always an honour to work with them and see them achieve so much more than they thought possible. I have worked with many types and levels of global leaders who have transformed their workplace and are achieving the personal success they deserve. I have also worked with people making that challenging first step into team leadership, some of whom are now working as CEOs of successful organisations.

My work is very pragmatic and hands on. Up to now this has been mainly in small groups on leadership journey programmes. This means I haven't worked with as many leaders as I would like to, and need to, if we are to get to a tipping point of change. This handbook is my humble attempt to work with many more great people like you to awaken possibility and change the way we lead.

So you are probably thinking why more people? I believe that so many people are unhappy at work because organisations are run by people using outdated mindsets and tools, causing organisations to be over managed and under led. My mission is to change that! My key purpose is to change the way organisations are led and awaken possibility in leaders like you to deliver extraordinary results. I have developed the leaders of many household brand names that you will know; many successful global brands, public sector organisations, social enterprise and smaller entrepreneurial businesses. I love sharing my thoughts and foresight into what makes a leader successful in today's world and well into the future. I love working with forward thinking people like you.

I am a family man at heart, love the sun on my skin and the sand in my toes, travelling, exercise and being with loved ones. I work globally and enjoy teaching Leadership, developing Senior Teams, creating Strategy, Business Modelling, Salesforce Transformation, Developing Elite Teams, Innovation and supporting leaders to be the best they can be.

This handbook is your access to my very latest leadership thinking about what great leaders do today - my life's work so far! It is packed full of ideas designed to support you in honing your leadership skills to ensure you get promoted, reduce stress, earn more income, have fun and give you the life you deserve. It will give you an insight into my values and what I believe we need to do to ensure a better world! In the spirit of abundance I have included tools I have learnt from others along my leadership journey and have found to be really useful in achieving great results.

I have had the honour to be described by clients as an 'igniter of human potential', a 'true leadership wizard,' an 'inspirational storyteller' and an 'inspirational provider of practical insights that make a difference – immediately'.

Meet me and find out more at grahamwilson.com

"LET'S CHANGE THE WAY ORGANISATIONS ARE LED."

GRAHAM WILSON

"GREAT LEADERS AWAKEN POSSIBILITY IN PEOPLE TO DELIVER EXTRAORDINARY RESULTS."

GRAHAM WILSON

CONTENTS

LEADERSHIP LAID BARE

THE NAKED TRUTH OF WHAT GREAT LEADERS ACTUALLY DO

"THEY CREATE A HIGH PERFORMANCE ENVIRONMENT WHERE SUCCESS IS INEVITABLE"

1 LEADERSHIP PURPOSE:
THEY AWAKEN POSSIBILITY IN PEOPLE TO DELIVER EXTRAORDINARY RESULTS

3 LEADERSHIP PRINCIPLES:
THEY OPERATE WITH BOLDNESS, SIMPLICITY AND SPEED

7 LEADERSHIP TRUTHS:
THEY LIVE THE 7 TIMELESS LEADERSHIP PRINCIPLES

1 THEY UNDERSTAND THEMSELVES AND HAVE A STORY TO TELL:
THEY HAVE AN AUTHENTIC LEADERSHIP BRAND, THEY BUILD ON STRENGTHS, THEY ARE HAPPY BEING VULNERABLE, THEY ARE THEMSELVES, THEY SHARE THEIR LEADERSHIP PHILOSOPHY, THEY BUILD TRUST, THEY ARE POSITIVE, HEALTHY AND HAPPY.

2 THEY INSPIRE ACTION:
PURPOSE IS AT THE HEART OF EVERYTHING THEY DO, THEY MAKE A DIFFERENCE, THEY HAVE COURAGE, THEY GO OUT ON A LIMB, THEY ARE BOLD, THEY TELL STORIES AND GIVE EXAMPLES THAT GIVE MEANING AND INSPIRE ACTION. THEY CREATE A SENSE OF REAL VALUE.

INNOVATION

TEAMWORK

4 THEY UNLEASH INNOVATION:
THEY CREATE A CULTURE WHERE EVERYONE COMES UP WITH GREAT IDEAS TO IMPROVE PERFORMANCE AND ADD VALUE. THEY INNOVATE IN EVERY ASPECT OF BUSINESS. THEY ARE RELENTLESS DISCOVERERS. THEY EXPLOIT TECHNOLOGY AND PLATFORMS.

5 THEY MANAGE AMBIGUITY AND KILL RISK:
THEY ARE COMFORTABLE WITH PARADOXES, MAKE THE COMPLEX SIMPLE, UNDERSTAND THE NEED FOR EVOLVING PLANS, THEY ARE AGILE. THEY ARE MENTALLY TOUGH AND RESILIENT TO DEAL WITH A WORLD IN PERPETUAL CRISIS. THEY ANTICIPATE AND KILL RISK QUICKLY. THEY STAY IN TOUCH WITH THE WORLD.

3 THEY CREATE HIGH PERFORMANCE TEAMS:
THEY ARE COMFORTABLE WITH COLLABORATION, EMPOWERMENT, AUTONOMY AND KNOW HOW TO BUILD TEAMS QUICKLY.

7 THEY DELIVER WITH PACE:
THEY TRANSLATE STRATEGY INTO MEANING AND INSPIRE ACTION, THEY JOIN THE DOTS, THEY ARE COMFORTABLE SPEEDING UP BY SLOWING DOWN, THEY DELIVER THROUGH PEOPLE AND TEAMS, THEY EXECUTE.

6 THEY EDUCATE:
THEY HELP PEOPLE AND ORGANISATIONS LEARN, THEY INSPIRE CURIOSITY, THEY ONLY TELL WHEN DIRECTION IS ABSOLUTELY NEEDED, THEY ENSURE LEARNING IS APPLIED, THEY LEAD WITH QUESTIONS, THEY COACH. THEY DEVELOP AND NURTURE CAPABILITY.

"WHEN I TALK TO MANAGERS I GET THE FEELING THAT THEY ARE IMPORTANT.

WHEN I TALK TO LEADERS I GET THE FEELING THAT I AM IMPORTANT."

ALEXANDER DEN HEIJER

WELCOME TO YOUR
TOTAL LEADERSHIP BLUEPRINT

Leadership Laid Bare is the fastest, easiest and most reliable system for improving your leadership capability, even if you are really busy!

You are holding a handbook for leadership visionaries and game changers; it's not for the faint hearted. It is for people who want to challenge the way organisations are led and want to make a contribution in leading the way.

WARNING, this book could **RADICALLY CHANGE** the way you **LEAD!**

This handbook is for you

Leadership applies to many aspects of our lives; be it at different levels at work, running your own business, being a parent or being a community leader. The same leadership principles apply to all. If you are a CEO of a global business who wouldn't read a book with pictures in it then this is definitely for you! If you are about to start your own business and grow it rapidly then this book is for you. If you are looking to progress quickly in your organisation then this is for you. If you are looking to improve your life this book is for you. Still not sure; then have a think about these questions:

- Are you fed up with the way organisations are led? Y/N

- Do you want to make a real difference in the world? Y/N

- Do you have a burning passion to unleash your potential? Y/N

- Do you feel restricted and want to reclaim your personal power? Y/N

- Do you feel you could achieve so much more? Y/N

- Do you want to craft a life on your own terms? Y/N

- Are you ready to enjoy happiness, wealth, health, achievement and contribution? Y/N

- Are you searching for a pragmatic way to change the way you lead? Y/N

- Have you realised that command and control doesn't cut it anymore? Y/N

- Do you want to improve your leadership skills and get promoted? Y/N

- Do you want to put the smile back on your face? Y/N

If you've answered yes to any of these questions then you will find this book really useful. See it as the combination to unlock your leadership success. Welcome to the Leadership Revolution!

"IMAGINE A WORLD WHERE PEOPLE WAKE UP AND FEEL INSPIRED TO GO TO WORK."

SIMON SINEK

It's time to change the way organisations are led

Have you noticed recently that so many people are unhappy at work? According to Gallup Research unhappy employees outnumber happy ones by two to one worldwide. There are twice as many "actively disengaged" workers in the world as there are "engaged" workers who love their jobs. How sad is that! Have you ever wondered why it is like that?

Why is it that so many people are stressed, overwhelmed, tired, unhealthy, unhappy, depressed, frustrated, disengaged, not enabled, want to do a great job but can't, not trusted, attend meetings that add no value, not listened to, not asked for ideas, and potentially victims of large egos and bullying? A sorry picture to start a book on leadership I know but sadly the reality in so many organisations around the world. We need to change that and we as leaders are accountable!

Why is it that with all the leadership books being read and courses being run it is still not working? Leaders are failing, perhaps we need a new way.

It isn't time for a leadership movement; it's time for a LEADERSHIP REVOLUTION! A revolution based on creating leaders who can awaken possibility in people to deliver extraordinary results. A revolution that creates leaders who know how to develop followers into leaders. A leadership revolution that changes the way organisations are led.

For many of us it is time to look squarely into the mirror, take a big breath, look through tired eyes and ask ourselves some tough question. Why am I distracted so much? Why is my life led by email? Why is my life so reactive? Why do I attend so many meetings that add no value? Why do I need all these measures and reports? Why am I so busy? Why do I feel so pressurised? Why does my style of management not work anymore?

I would like to invite you on a magical leadership journey. A journey that will help you understand why we need a new breed of leaders, how your past can stop you from being successful, how great leaders inspire action and deliver extraordinary results, and more importantly share with you what you specifically need to do to develop your leadership capability even if you are busy!

I have been lucky enough to work with tens of thousands of amazing leaders and organisations to develop my craft and hone my skills. I am now ready to share that with you. I will share with you tried, tested and proven leadership tools that I have taught over the past 21 years to create significant organisational and personal success on a global scale.

With so much to cover, let's get started.

Your leadership journey:

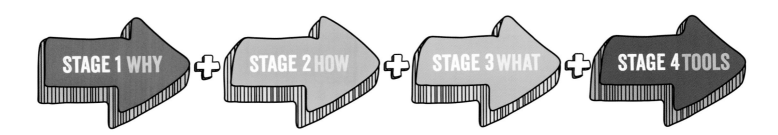

Why we need to change

The internal mindsets getting in our way

The external changes driving change

Exploring how great leaders lead

Role of a Leader

Purpose of Leadership

Leadership Principles

The 7 Truths

What to do to improve

4 step process to improve your leadership capability

Your leadership tools

A range of practical leadership tools to use straight away

How to get the most from this handbook

Just before we leap into learning about leadership let me share with you how to get the best from your investment.

I have written this handbook as if I am talking to you and you alone. This handbook is for **you!** Find a great place to relax and let's get into the conversation around leadership and improving your results. Remember that the real value from this handbook comes from the moment you put it down and start acting on your insights and ideas.

I recommend thinking about your leadership challenges before you go any further. I know you are excited about getting started but think for a while about what challenges you face. Talk to your peers, your boss, your partner, your friends and then turn your challenges into a series of leadership questions.

Such as:
What does a successful leader actually do in today's world?
How do I get my team really engaged and enabled for success?
How do I create a culture of innovation?
How do I get the organisation to understand and act on the strategy?
How do I kill complexity?

Make your goal finding the answers to your questions. Read the handbook and search for your answers, they will be there!

I have used the style of layout in the handbook for a purpose. It gives you plenty of white space and areas to record your thoughts, so take notes as you read it. This will really help you with creating your plan of action.

When I teach leadership programmes face to face I share a great three stage mental model you can use to ensure the best outcomes are achieved:

Learn by reading this book with an open mind writing down your insights and golden nuggets as they arrive. **Connect** at an emotional level to the stories, examples and messages as you read. What does this mean in your world? Have you experienced this before? Do you know this, and do you apply it? Reread the book and add to your ideas and then **Act** by creating an evolving plan.

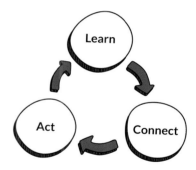

I have included areas in the book at the end of each section to help you with this and a few questions to prompt your thinking.

Remember that this book is written from my experiences, my learning, my thoughts and my aspirations. It is important for you to test what I am saying, connect with it from your world and only apply what feels right for you. Most of all have fun solving YOUR leadership questions in YOUR way!

"THE REASON PEOPLE ARE SO UNHAPPY AT WORK IS THAT MANAGERS ARE BEING TRAINED FOR A WORLD THAT DOESN'T EXIST ANYMORE. I WANT TO CHANGE THAT!"

GRAHAM WILSON

STAGE 1 WHY

STAGE 1: WHY

Awakening Possibility: Why we need to change the way we lead and what gets in the way.

In order to change the way we behave we need to fully understand why we need to change. Once we have fully understood the why and the barriers we need to overcome, then change will happen.

"LEADERSHIP AND LEARNING ARE INDISPENSABLE TO EACH OTHER."

JOHN F KENNEDY

Why we need to change the way we lead

I believe the best learning comes from stories and experimentation. When was the last time you had that moment of shift when it all suddenly made sense? Probably after a story or an example and some mindfulness.

To challenge your thinking I'd like to start our time together with a series of short stories that illustrate the sometimes very strange and non-logical behaviour we experience when leaders lead! Examples of these strange behaviours are:

- Managers running update meetings that are a waste of time and destroy trust
- Running meetings that add no value to the participants
- Insisting that people spend time filling out reports when they should be serving their customers
- Managers destroying confidence in their teams
- Managers stuck on deliverables and not spending time building teams and relying on the ad hoc "away day" to sort it
- Managers covering their fears with control and pretend behaviour

Based on these examples and your own experiences I'm sure you'll agree with me that many organisations are over managed and under led.

I find many managers get stuck in control, strategy, plans and KPIs. Typical examples of how this shows up are the paternalistic way managers lead people by feeling that they have to be the rescuer, managers having all the answers and telling people what to do, the absence of trust in the work place, over complication, bureaucracy running wild, KPIs everywhere and thousands of meetings that add no value and destroy trust.

Can you relate to this in your world?

Imagine if you were having some decorating done at home and you decide to pop back at lunch time and the decorators are having a meeting, filling out forms and on their mobiles doing emails; would you be happy?

Let's explore together why this happens and what you can do about it.

KILLER MINDSETS:
WHAT SCHOOL TAUGHT
US ABOUT LEADERSHIP.

1. Teamwork is CHEATING - or is it?

Let's go back to your classroom to an experience we have all probably had. When your teacher asked you a question, how did you respond? Normally what happens is you think about the question and if you know the answer you stick your hand up in the hope that your teacher will ask you to share your knowledge. This repeated pattern of behaviour starts our need for recognition and reward, "me miss, me, me, ask me, I know!" I wonder what would have happened if you had turned around to your classmates and tried to have dialogue and discussion around the question, what would the teacher have done? If you went to a school like mine then the teacher would have told you off, told you to be quiet or even reported you and sent you to the headmaster as you continued to be a disruptive member of the class. Think for a moment how that plays out in your work and your behaviour today.

I can remember we had a woodwork teacher who used to throw woodworking chisels at you if you didn't have the answer or did something wrong in his view and I can remember them sticking in the wall behind me. So when you think about it, what we were taught at school is that teamworking and collaboration is cheating! Isn't that an interesting reflection on what is required in today's world? Added to this when you were at school who was the person who had the final answer? It was the teacher. So we also believe it is good to always have the answers.

As we get promoted to become managers what have we just become? A teacher. It is easy to fall into the trap as a leader that teamwork is cheating and that we need to be the solution providers. I was coaching a project manager from a global organisation who was running multi million, high risk, visible projects and struggling. They had cost overruns happening, customers not happy with the wrong things being delivered, missing deadlines - not a great picture. When we explored the challenge we found that it was their inability to build teams that was causing the problems. He was too busy doing the work himself. He had no time to manage stakeholders and make the ongoing changes required to the project. Once I coached him how to build and run project teams and shared collaboration techniques, the world was a great place again.

Questions for you:
Have you fallen into the trap of solving problems and telling? Do you try and come up with the answers and then hold meetings to inform people what to do? Do you fall into the trap of silo mentality, not collaborating, not building alliances and partnerships, not using open innovation techniques and not utilising the power of your team?

2. It's all about PERFECTION - or is it?

Do you remember getting your school report? If like me, there was probably one subject you didn't like or didn't care about. Probably because the teacher didn't inspire you or ignite your passion around the subject. Imagine getting your school report and in every other subject apart from the one you hate you get a fantastic mark. You don't care about the one poor result as you don't like the subject so you go home feeling really proud about a good year and excited to share that with your parents. You come home and you lay your school report on the dining room table to share. What would be the first thing they would say? Let me guess - I bet they said, "What happened there then?" Pointing out the one poor result, ignoring all the fantastic results you achieved in the other subjects. Am I right?

So how does this play out in work? If like many organisations you have score cards and everything is fantastic apart from one red dot, I wonder what you focus on with your team? It wouldn't be all the green dots I'm sure, it's going to be the one red dot that catches your attention. If you think back to how you felt at home with your parents I wonder how you make your team feel?

Perhaps we need to focus on what is important, not just the red dots.

Questions for you:
Where do you focus your attention? What feeling and culture are you creating in yourself and your team?

3. Make sure you measure RESULTS - or should it be RESULTS and PERFORMANCE?

Whilst I'm thinking about KPIs, I wonder how many of your KPIs are really KPIs? I have found that in many organisations they are actually MRIs - Many Result Indicators! When KPIs first came out the first word was KEY. What are the 2, 3, 4, 5 maximum actions you want people to focus on. The P was about PERFORMANCE. What is it that you actually want them to do. Today most indicators are focussed on results rather than inputs. What this can do if we are not careful is create performance anxiety.

The challenge with this is that when we are anxious and stressed we go into flight or fight response. Now to protect us what happens is that our thinking part of the brain switches off. Think and you are dead, you get eaten by the sabre tooth tiger! Which is exactly the same as when we try to reward people with bonuses? More about that later! So this over reliance on MRIs is actually reducing performance and results in our business.

How would you feel if you were recruited because of your massive talent and experience and your boss says to you, "We really welcome you to the business, great to have you on board it's great that you have all this experience and talent but I am going to measure you just to check up on your performance. Oh and by the way we'll have a monthly update meeting where I will check up on you and on your KPIs. "I wonder how you would feel and how trusted you felt? Wouldn't it be great if managers would trust people with talent and experience! And they got out of the way!

Questions for you:
What do you measure - just results or results and performance?
Are you creating performance anxiety?

4. You must CONTROL everything - or do you?

I read in the papers a few years ago about a story of mum and a little girl. They were walking past a doctor's surgery and the little girl tripped and fell over gashing her forehead on the brick wall around the surgery. Being outside the surgery, the traumatised mum picked the girl up rushed into the surgery and was met by a receptionist who said, "I am really sorry but we can't treat you here because you are not registered." How can that happen? The poor lady and the little girl had to run up the street for over a mile to get to their own GP service to get one of the nurses to treat the facial wound, and as you know facial wounds bleed an awful lot. So I wonder how this has happened? I can imagine in a Practice meeting that the manager has said to the staff, "If no one is registered you cannot treat them." The tragedy is if we create an over controlled and over managed environment people stop thinking. Many organisations are stuck in management and strategy and play this out with over control.

Let me share another story that I heard René Carayol talk about in one of his leadership conferences. It was about a lady who was trapped in a building that had collapsed. She had her phone with her and managed to press last number redial. The phone call was to a bank. Within three rings she was talking to a human being.

The lady shared that she was trapped and was losing consciousness and could they put her through to her husband and also her children. The operator sprang into action and whilst keeping the lady talking to keep her conscious she arranged for one of her colleagues to contact her husband and one of her other colleagues to contact her children and the third operator to contact the emergency services. The lady was eventually rescued and reunited with her husband and children – a lovely happy ending.

How did that happen? The leaders of the organisation had created the right culture. Your role as a leader is to create the right culture. You don't create a good culture by over managing and controlling everything – that is when people stop thinking and do stupid things. You do it by creating a high performance environment where success is inevitable and allowing people to think and perform.

Questions for you:
What culture are you creating? Are you stopping people from thinking and acting?

5. It's all about being BUSY - or is it?

In today's busy world I am guessing as a manager and a leader in your organisation you are really busy. I grew up with my father racing motorbikes and my uncle racing motor cars and my grandmother had a sweet/toy shop. What a great childhood! When I listened to my dad and my uncle talking about winning races and the reason why they lost races; a pattern emerged. The reason they lost races was because they were going too fast, normally spinning out of a corner and crashing. In business we are taught to have a "can do" busy culture when the real secret is knowing when to go fast and when to slow down. You could say in order to speed up we need to slow down.

So in business let me ask you when do you make your mistakes? Is it when you are calm, collected and in control or when you are really really busy? Usually it is when you are really busy. So let me ask when is it the best time to stop, slow down and review? When you are busy. When is the one time we never slow down and review? When we're busy. We all know that planning is important, we all know that the execution of the plan is important, and we all know that we should continually improve our performance but for some reason we don't review and learn enough in business today.

Questions for you:
Do you speed up by slowing down? Do you keep things on track by regular review and do you learn effectively with your team?

6. You must be a HERO - or do you?

I was with a team a while ago and I asked them to split into two groups and draw a model of how they operate in their business. So the teams disappeared off and had some great dialogue and discussion. When they presented back their thoughts the first team presented a cyclical model which started with 'do' and the 2nd stage was 'do' 3rd stage was 'do' and I bet you can guess what the 4th stage was - yes you are right, do!

They called this their 'hamster wheel' so their work routine was work really hard to the point that the hamster wheel is going really fast, a bit too fast and then you book a two week holiday. The first week you are ill because you have been working too hard and your immune system has broken down and the second week you are worried about what's happening in the work place. When you get back someone has been pushing your hamster wheel and it is faster than when you left. Normally indicated by the volume of emails you have waiting for you on your return, and your immediate thoughts go to needing another holiday. Or you think going on holiday is too much hassle and creates too much work.

The second team came back with their model and started by saying they have created all by themselves a 'busy' culture. It doesn't matter what you are doing as long as you are busy you'll be okay. When you are busy of course that's when the mistakes get made, so the second stage was 'fire-fighting', rushing around trying to put fires out but not enough time to put them out properly before having to go and put another fire out somewhere else. The third stage was 'blame'. This is what human beings tend to do to off load the accountability by blaming something or someone. By blaming we remove the need to change, so the fourth stage was 'nothing changes' and we go back to being busier. They have created a culture which says, "Don't solve a problem on a Monday when you can solve a crisis on a Friday."

The reason being is they have created a concept called hero worship. If you rush in and save the business and turn the red KPIs into green ones then you are seen as a hero and promoted. The people who never let their projects, pieces of work, function, team get into crisis never get noticed because their score cards are always green.

I'm sure you can guess which type of leader is successful in today's world, not a hero!

Questions for you:
Are you a hero? If yes how are you going to change that?

7. Plan everything in DETAIL - or do you?

A few years ago I was asked to help out a project team as they were struggling with putting together a project plan. They had been told by their bosses that they had to put a complete end to end plan together to enable the senior managers to decide whether they could let the project go ahead. Sound familiar? The team were struggling because the project was a bit vague in terms of what they should be doing to achieve the benefits they wanted. They knew they had a problem, weren't really sure what the cause of the problem was and didn't know how to fix it.

Yet in this context their leaders still wanted to see a detailed project plan so they could monitor and control the project. It is no wonder that so many change initiatives and projects fail. What was needed was a collaborative and evolving approach to making the change happen. Planning in detail was a waste of time and actually creating more risk than taking a more agile approach.

A few years ago I was working with a client who was looking to open up in China. They had spent 5 years trying to develop new products to launch and were failing miserably. They were looking for the perfect answer. Just like the previous example they needed the complete project plan before starting.

When they discovered that an evolving approach is a great strategy in today's world they took what they had and tried it out. They just went and set up with their partner.

Some products failed, some were ok, and some did really well. They reviewed often, worked in a collaborative way, put controls in place and learnt plenty. In a couple of years they achieved a thriving and growing business in China. If they hadn't changed their approach they would still be trying to develop the perfect products and launch plan for China.

It happens in the day to day work of organisations as well. It amazes me how many businesses still put so much control through annual budgets. I once experienced seeing a manager buying product from a local store out of her own pocket because she had run out of budget on that line on her excel spreadsheet. She knew what would happen if she went over, and knew she needed the product for her customers, so she spent her own money!

We are using ways of working that are outdated and too slow in today's fast paced, volatile, uncertain, complex and ambiguous world. When your company has spent millions on creating the annual budget, what is the one thing you know? It is wrong and will need changing! And we do this every year! How many of you have had to plan a project in detail just to get authorisation to do it? Then had to change everything.

Questions for you:
Are you comfortable with emerging and evolving plans? Are you happy with breaking down projects into steps? Are you happy with just knowing the first actions? Do you set up a collaborative and learning culture?

8. Organise in functions - or should you?

Have you ever wondered why we have set up our education system based on Industrial Age thinking? Let me ask you a question, "What locations were the subjects at your school taught? Were they in different classrooms and taught by different specialist teachers? How are old world MBAs taught? Module 1 - Strategy, Module 2 - Marketing, Module 3 - Finance, etc. With different professors running each session, probably saying that their subject is the most important!

Guess how we organise our businesses? We put all the sales people together, the finance people together, the marketing people together, the engineers together, IT people in the dungeon (only joking) - you get the picture. We then install heads of departments to further embed the silo mentality. Why do we do that? Maybe it's because we feel we need control and order.

The problem now is that the world doesn't work like that, it is all interconnected. Wouldn't it be great if our children were taught in a way that supports a globalised interconnected world? Wouldn't it be great if we were taught to do maths, languages, geography and history in one go and were showed, or we worked out, how they all interconnected? Wouldn't it be great when our organisations are structured like that?

Questions for you:
Have you created a silo mentality? If so how can you become more collaborative? Could you restructure the way you do things? Could you become more agile?

What can stop you changing

Learning and growth requires courage to
overcome your fears and unleash the
REAL YOU ...

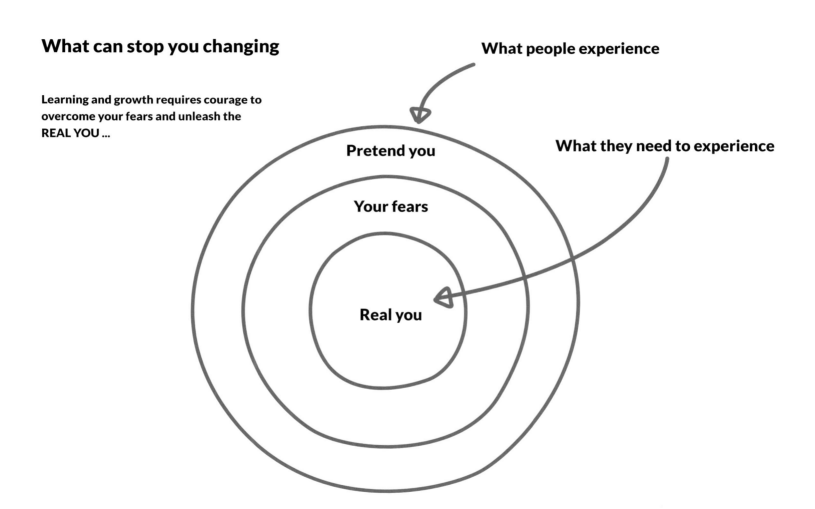

What people experience

What they need to experience

Pretend you

Your fears

Real you

Taking Action: Next steps is overcoming your mindset challenges

I was in the park on a beautiful fun packed day with my sister's grandchildren and as we had great fun exploring and playing and learning I heard very interesting comments from other parents in the park. "Suzy don't do that you will fall off and hurt yourself" and "Get down right now, that is too dangerous" and "No that is too high for you." Hmm I wonder how these children will behave when they grow up? No encouragement, no choice of words to focus the children's minds to be safe and achieve success, not a single word. Without knowing it we become resistant to change because of fear of doing something wrong. To illustrate this I do a quick exercise with the groups I am teaching. Let's do it now. If you put your book down and join your hands together so your fingers are interlinked. You will find that you have a bias of which way around you do it. You may have your right hand higher or your left.

If you change your hands around how does it feel? Very strange?

Added to the fear built into us we also like what feels familiar. Change requires energy and focus to make it happen. If you change your hands around about twenty times the brain now doesn't know which is the normal way and feels comfortable either way - go on try it! Fear is the key destroyer of change and greatness.

In order to reduce fear and turn it to our advantage we need to look at it as fun in disguise. We need to tame and master it. Sure fear is a great way to switch on the receptors of danger, but let it take hold, it can stop you in your tracks.

Fear used to be used to protect us from being eaten alive by sabre tooth tigers and the like. Yet today it can be the product of social conditioning, fear of being rejected, feeling ugly, being embarrassed, not being perfect or failing. It comes from comments like, don't climb that you will fall off and hurt yourself, that's not for the likes of us, you can't do that. It comes from years of teachers, coaches and managers focussing on all the mistakes you make.

How many times have you had a situation where you have had a fantastic year and in your review the one thing your manager talks about is the one little mistake you made - thought so! We need to break free from our limiting mindsets and break into reclaiming our personal freedom.

This handbook is designed to help you do just that and guess what, you have already achieved stage one; raising awareness for the need for change.

Summary: Our mindsets are killing our success

Negative beliefs:

- The belief that you as a leader have to have the answers
- The belief that you are the adult, the teacher that being paternalistic is the way forward
- The belief that being busy is good
- The belief that you have to be perfect
- The belief that you have to control through measuring everything
- The belief that just managing works rather than managing and leading

- The belief that you must be a hero
- The belief that the detailed plan is the most important thing
- The belief that leadership comes from the top
- The belief that the people above you know the answers
- The belief that you can't get it wrong
- The belief that you have to be really careful
- The belief that you have to fit in

Positive beliefs:

- The belief that you enable the answer
- The belief that people can solve their own problems with your support
- The belief that being effective is good
- The belief that good is good enough
- The belief that you can trust people to get on
- The belief that you need to manage and lead
- The belief that you don't need to be a hero

- The belief that emerging plans work best
- The belief that leadership comes from the front, side and back
- The belief that the people nearest the problem have the answers
- The belief that fast failure is good
- The belief that risk is good when planned
- The belief that being yourself and speaking your mind with skill, is important

Great leaders take MASSIVE action:
Now is your opportunity to develop your plan of action

Learn: My key learnings are:

_____

_____

_____

_____

Connect: What this means for me is:

_____

_____

_____

_____

Act: What I'm going to do is:

_____

_____

_____

_____

"LEADERS TRANSMIT THEIR ENERGY... ...PEOPLE THEN DECIDE."

GRAHAM WILSON

Apart from our own mindsets, what else is stopping us being effective?

Our world has changed. Did you notice and evolve? It's not just the wrong mindsets that give us problems when leading. There are external factors driving the need for a change in the way we lead.

Have you noticed that planning seems to be different now, budgets are always out of date, there is more ambiguity, things happen quicker, change is the only constant! We need to constantly do more with less.

Added to the internal mindsets that drive our behaviour there are external factors contributing to a need for a new breed of leaders. During my military career I worked with the US Marines and Army. They talked about a VUCA world. I had no idea what it meant at the time, I do now! Our New World (VUCA world) is characterised by:

Volatility   The nature, speed, volume, magnitude and dynamics of change;

Uncertainty   The lack of predictability of issues and events;

Complexity   The confounding of issues and the chaos that surround any organisation; and

Ambiguity   The haziness of reality and the mixed meanings of conditions.

The challenge we have is that leaders are struggling with how best to lead in different conditions. They are struggling because many are still using outdated techniques in a changed context.

We have all experienced the pace of change increasing and how that is impacting on our lives. You just need to think about how technology development is speeding up and how that is changing behaviours. I only have to look at the behaviour of my children to see it. Social media, smart phones, and the internet have driven new ways of operating. The predictions are that the pace of change will get even faster - very soon!

Most leaders recognise that they need to change if they are going to prosper in our new environment, the challenge is what to change to.

Thankfully through my work I have experienced what great looks like in today's world and I would like to share my thoughts with you.

"IF THE RATE OF CHANGE ON THE OUTSIDE EXCEEDS THE RATE OF CHANGE ON THE INSIDE, THE END IS NEAR."

JACK WELCH

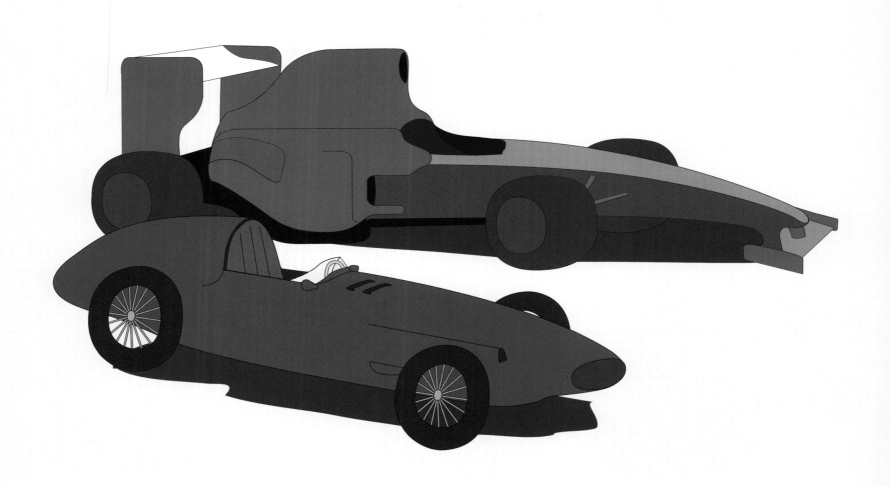

Our world has changed

I remember being told in my early military career that we were training soldiers for a war that hasn't been fought yet. We have no idea what they will be doing, what technology, what weapons, or in what locations they will be fighting or protecting; but we need to get them ready!

In today's world we need to train leaders for now and the future. The question is, how do we do that if it hasn't happened yet? My personal views on that is that we clarify the expectations of a leader and create leaders who can think for themselves and craft solutions for messy problems. Leaders who can adapt rapidly, learn quickly, keep agile and thrive in an ever changing workplace.

In the 1950s it took approximately 4 minutes to do a pit stop for a racing car. What is it now in F1? The car barely stops these days! In the 1950s the rules were different than they are now but F1 teams have adapted and changed the way they do it based on the new rules, learning and technology available.

The challenge we have in business is that many people haven't recognised that the rules have changed and that they need to lead in a different way. They are using out dated tools and techniques in a different context. Imagine if you turned up at a F1 pitstop today with your cotton trousers and shirt, a big lump hammer to remove the locking nuts, a cloth to wipe the windscreen, a cup of tea for the driver, and a bit of fuel!

You would have looked great in the 1950s but hey ... a bit out of place in a F1 team today!

So why is it today that many leaders turn up to work with their outdated ways of working and think it is ok to behave this way?

The 7 dysfunctions of a leader

DYSFUNCTIONAL LEADERSHIP

Unauthentic: hide their fears with pretend behaviour

Use coercive power to force people to follow

Build low trust working groups

Micro manage the status quo

Use "hero" behaviour by being reactive

Save people by telling and informing

Line manage in silos

THIS DOESN'T WORK ANYMORE

SUCCESSFUL LEADERSHIP

100% Authentic: bring their real self to work

Inspire a movement by being purpose led and a great story teller.

Build high performance teams; quickly

Innovate in all that they do

Manage ambiguity and risk by being proactive

Educate and develop people

Execute with speed cross functionally

THIS WORKS NOW!

"EVERYTHING YOU WANT IS ON THE OTHER SIDE OF FEAR."

JACK CANFIELD

STAGE 1 WHY + STAGE 2 HOW

STAGE 2: HOW

The naked truth about what makes a great leader in today's world?

Have you ever wondered why some leaders inspire action and others don't? How some leaders turn followers into leaders and deliver extraordinary results; whilst others get stuck in management control and mediocrity? Have you debated in your mind what the true role of a leader is, what the purpose of leadership is, what the key principles are, and what successful leaders actually do on a day to day basis to be successful?
Let's explore what I believe to be the truth.

"IF YOUR ACTIONS INSPIRE OTHERS TO DREAM MORE, LEARN MORE, DO MORE, AND BECOME MORE; YOU ARE A LEADER."

JOHN QUINCY ADAMS

The naked truth about what makes a great leader in today's world

We now know that our internal mindsets, beliefs and values could be holding us back and that the pace of change is requiring a change. The question is, "How do we lead in today's world?"

In a very volatile, very uncertain, very complex, very challenging and very ambiguous world we need new skills and behaviours. From a leadership point of view it means that in the old world where things were pretty stable and we didn't need to change much; the way we led was to create a command and control structure.

We made sure that the people who had the knowledge were at the top of the organisation and they had probably done the job before and they knew exactly what to do in the business. They could operate from experience because they had done the job before, been there, seen it, got the t-shirt, got the certificate.

The world hadn't changed so when they did the job it had been the same for the last 20 years so we looked to our management team really as experts, controllers, managers of status quo. If you had a problem go and speak to your manager and they would tell you what to do. We installed functions, reports, plans, objectives to ensure people did what we as managers wanted.

Another thing we learnt is that with all the knowledge being at the top of the business then clearly they should be the people who make the decisions. When you needed help, who would you ask for help - your boss. The implication was that people higher up the organisation had the answers; this is not the case in our today's world.

With a command and control mindset what used to happen was that we would create a reporting system where the people doing the real work, adding the real value for our customers, the real money earning operations would report up to their managers who would then report up to their managers. Of course everyone obviously wanted to do very well so what they would do was make sure their report looked really good, shiny and perfect. Then send it up to the next level and of course they'd do exactly the same.

What would happen is all this data would go up to the top of the business and the people at the top of the business would make the decisions, create a plan or a strategy and then cascade that down through their briefing system and this worked. It worked really well when the pace of change was very slow. We used to lead from knowledge, we used to lead from experience. We would lead from the top of the organisation, we would lead by telling people what to do.

The problem is that it doesn't work like that anymore. This approach is too slow in today's world and it is dangerous when you make decisions based on the wrong data, by the wrong people.

"WHEN THE WINDS OF CHANGE BLOW, SOME PEOPLE BUILD WALLS WHILE OTHERS BUILD WINDMILLS."

CHINESE PROVERB

Discover the timeless leadership principles for the 21st Century

When you move forward from the past and into the world that we now operate in, then things start to change. The people at the top don't have the answers, they don't have the expertise, they don't have the knowledge and they don't have the experience because the world has changed so fast. When they did the job it was completely different to the people doing it now. We are now in a world needing more collaboration and more autonomy. We need to really push the decision making process down to the people who have the information and I think really that's one of the key leadership needs now.

We need to create a high performance culture where success is inevitable. What that means is we need to get our teams capable of making decisions, we need them thinking and doing - not just doing! They need the skills, confidence, knowledge and mindset to want to make it happen. If we continue to control we will stop people thinking.

Of course we need to set boundaries and guidelines to support this. We are now purpose maximisers. We need to lead a purposeful organisation where we make a promise to our customers. We need to ensure our people understand why we do business, the value we add to our customers, and the purpose of our business. They need to understand the goals that we are aiming to achieve, a set of values that are aligned to our purpose and goals. This framework really helps them to make decisions really quickly and effectively. It enables them to be operating with clarity and autonomy.

In today's world leadership is really around making sure we can build teams to fix problems, we can lead without knowing the answers, we can lead through ambiguity, we have an agile approach to our leadership style, we anticipate more, we can flex our style, we kill risks when they arise not when they cause problems and we are operating from the front rather than from the top. We need a new set of skills that we develop as leaders.

To help you achieve clarity on what to do as a leader I have created a leadership system; a Leadership Manifesto, a guideline, a blueprint; a step by step approach to help you to really get clarity in this ambiguous world.

I have broken the system down into a number of phases. The first stage is to really understand what the role of a leader is, then to understand the purpose of leadership and really give you some guidelines and a set of principles of how to operate.

The final part of the jigsaw is what I believe the 7 Leadership Truths actually are. What is it that leaders should be doing on a day to day basis, what are their work routines, their ways of working. The routines that are second nature and just happen.

"THE ROLE OF A LEADER IN TODAY'S WORLD IS TO CREATE A HIGH PERFORMANCE ENVIRONMENT WHERE SUCCESS IS INEVITABLE."

GRAHAM WILSON

Discover the timeless leadership principles for the 21st Century

Let's start with the Role of a Leader.

I believe the **role of a leader is to create a high performance environment where success is inevitable.** Create is a big word here. In the past we would set frameworks, we would create departments, functions, silos, and we would create a very rigid command and control structure that was very stable. In today's world we need to create a more flexible and agile structure where we have a core guiding coalition of people who guide the organisation in the right direction and we have teams of people with the right skill sets and we create teams really, really quickly to go out there and grab opportunities or to overcome challenges that we are facing.

What that means is we don't have a stable environment in which to work so in order to be successful as a leader I think creating a high performance environment is really important. We need to have the ability to be able to very quickly create the right culture, the right environment where the team will operate to achieve the right results and create the right performance culture to achieve the results we are looking for.

High performance of course is not just a great place to work. I have strong reservations about a great place to work because I certainly know from working in elite teams in the forces and with sports teams that a high performance culture is sometimes not a great place to work – it's challenging, its rigorous, it's hard, it's very rewarding and creates a great sense of pride and achievement. Not just a lovely place to work.

For me it is around creating a high challenge and high support environment. An environment where you push the boundaries on a day to day basis and people are striving to be better every single day.

The final part of the leadership role statement is "where success is inevitable." It is a really important aspect in today's world because things are changing so fast, we are in a more volatile and uncertain world, risks are increased. There are so many large organisations who fail dramatically in today's world – Nokia, Kodak, Borders to name a few; all cascading into failure rapidly. One of the reasons why this happens is that we don't manage risk in the right way.

In the past we got away with having risk workshops, analysing risks – creating wonderful matrixes, and spread sheets and mitigating the risks and creating good action plans but then the action plans sadly disappeared into someone's folder on their computer and no one knew anything about it until the risk came out and started to kill the project or the piece of work. We then rushed in on our white horses and saved the project or piece of work and became heroes and everything was fantastic.

In today's world what we need is leaders who have the time and can create the time to really anticipate the future and start to understand what could go wrong and create a path where they are anticipating the what ifs, they are anticipating the risks and they are killing the risk before it happens. Having time to think about really what could go wrong and make sure it doesn't go wrong requires a completely different way to look at risk than we perhaps did before.

The role of a leader is to create this high performance culture where success is inevitable - do you?

"THERE IS NO PASSION TO BE FOUND IN SETTLING FOR A LIFE THAT IS LESS THAN THE ONE YOU ARE CAPABLE OF LIVING."

NELSON MANDELA

Discover the timeless leadership principles for the 21st Century

What is the purpose of leadership?

For me the purpose of leadership is to awaken possibility in people to deliver extraordinary results. Let me repeat this as it is your foundation for success - **to awaken possibility in people to deliver extraordinary results**. What that means is that leadership is about "being." It is about role modelling and creating a high performance team. It is about understanding people and building trust. It is about building confidence in people so they can deliver amazing results. I see in so many over managed/under led organisations where the role of the manager seems to be to destroy confidence, to destroy people and to ensure they're disengaged and unable to achieve great results. I think we need to flip that around and start to focus our leaders on the individuals and the teams that are there to deliver the results we need. For me that is about coaching performance . It's all about developing people, helping them to learn, helping them to grow and realise that they can achieve so much more than they think is possible. I would like to propose that the key purpose of a leader is to make sure they challenge people, they work with people and they awaken the possibility in their people and help them to achieve extraordinary results.

Guiding Principles

Any revolution needs a manifesto and a manifesto needs some simple guiding principles. Here are the three core principles I think are vital for your leadership success: boldness, simplicity and speed.

Boldness

During the financial crisis in 2008 no issue has aroused more passion and energy than financial institution bailouts. I'm sure years of the wrong government policies added to the disaster but why did the banks behave the way they did up to the crisis? My personal view on this is that the banks were set up on a command and control fear based culture with low trust. I believe they had created a culture where people were too scared to say, "No we shouldn't be doing this, it is too risky." I think greed and fear took over. No one was bold enough to say no, let's not do this. One of the key aspects of being a great leader is being of ethical service, to serve others. Boldness is the willingness to take risks in the service of what matters, such as your organisational purpose, goals and values. It means being courageous, confronting, speaking out and acting in the face of fear and danger.

We need leaders who can operate with boldness. Being bold and courageous is not about being 'gung ho.' For me it's around being on purpose, honest, value led, being open, being able to speak your mind, being able to say what's in your thoughts. I know that when I was in the military I would rather have someone say that they couldn't do something, or that they were ill or injured rather than to think they are being courageous in saying, yes, yes I can do that and then let me down in the field when the bullets are flying. I definitely wouldn't want that to happen. For me being courageous is about people going out there being bold and being comfortable with vulnerability to do what is right.

"IF YOU CAN'T EXPLAIN IT TO A SIX YEAR OLD, YOU DON'T UNDERSTAND IT YOURSELF."

ALBERT EINSTEIN

Discover the timeless leadership principles for the 21st Century

Being bold of course is also about thinking big. It is about creating a good personal risk profile and making sure you can actually go for it as you test things out. You are comfortable failing fast if needed. So thinking big is a great principle I would propose for leaders in this New World. We now work in environments where things haven't been done before so I think that the old way universities teach people through case studies is redundant now. I believe it is around looking into the future, being bold, creating new ways of operating and really having the comfortable mindset of "OK I am going to go for it; if it fails I can kill risk quickly and develop new ways of doing things." So being bold is a key principle.

Simplicity

I was working with an organisation that used a big consultancy firm to develop their new Leadership Model. Theoretically and intellectually it was great and stacked up to the criteria and must have cost the tax payers a fortune! In my view it was too over engineered and complicated, they got so wrapped up in showing people how clever they were by creating such a complex model they forgot it had to be implemented by busy people. We need to keep things simple, not complicate or overburden our people. I see so many complicated strategies and plans that are so clever but can't be operationalised because they are so complex. I am a big fan of strategy on a page, plans on a page, projects on a page - you get the idea. You really have to understand what you are doing to put a complex situation on one page and remember the purpose of plans, to guide action! I've found the planning process is more important than the plan.

In a complex world it makes sense to be able to deal with complexity and make things simple. I stagger at the complexity organisations build into their ways of working. How over complex is your business?

Think about your business, think about the function or team that you lead and ask yourself what is it I can do to make it simple. How can I get rid of the millions of KPIs and the confusion that we create with the bureaucracy, the form filling, the report making, the overly complex process - all the things that make the job really challenging.

Let's get rid of those and keep it simple. What is it we actually need to do to make it successful? I have a belief that people tend not to remember more than three or four things anyway so what is it that I want them to focus on that really drives the performance and results.

Yet many companies I work with say, "Well, you don't understand; our business is really complicated." My belief is that it is not complex, they just make it complicated. I think this comes from this whole mindset of, "If I am working in a complex organisation then I am really intelligent which means I am more successful." All we are doing really is boosting our egos when we just need to make the business simple.

"SPEED IS OFTEN CONFUSED WITH BEING BUSY. YOU CAN SPEED UP BY SLOWING DOWN."

GRAHAM WILSON

Speed

I was working with a large retailer who were going through a major change programme. The organisation was funded by venture capitalists, the pressure was on. Sadly they could not make the change quick enough and the investors got bullish, the leadership team were replaced.

So, let's make things simple: we've got Boldness, we've got Simplicity and the third thing in today's world is we have got to operate with Pace. We have got to deliver quickly, we've got to execute around priorities, and we've got to make sure that we know how to take a strategy and then take the strategy and turn it into a plan, and then operationalise it really quickly. We need to create a sense of urgency.

One client I work with has achieved this by creating a culture of perpetual crisis. It certainly keeps leaders on their toes and constantly innovating.

We also need to be comfortable with this whole concept of speeding up by slowing down – we know when to go fast, we know when to slow down we know when to review, reflect and learn. We know that there is a big difference between a plan and the planning process. We know how to engage people, we know how to get teams on board quickly and we can execute with immense speed. This is a crucial element in today's world.

I am amazed by this whole concept of 10 year plans, 5 year plans and the annual planning process. I believe we need to start to operate in smaller time frames whilst still keeping an eye on the future and what is coming. We need to speed up our delivery by taking an evolving approach and operating with greater pace. Let's start operating in 90 day planning cycles and keeping an eye on the future visions.

To summarise, we have seen that the role of a leader is to create a high performance environment where success is inevitable. We've talked about the purpose of leadership being the need to awaken possibility in people to deliver extraordinary results and we have described the three principles of Boldness, Simplicity and Pace.

So what is it that a leader does on a day to day basis?

I have called these **The 7 LEADERSHIP TRUTHS** - let's explore.

"GREAT LEADERS TURN FOLLOWERS INTO LEADERS WHO DELIVER EXTRAORDINARY RESULTS."

GRAHAM WILSON

The 7 Leadership Truths

When you strip leadership down to the fundamentals it is a simple process. One person transmits their energy and then the other person/people make a decision. If they follow then the other person is a leader. I have discovered 7 Leadership Truths that when part of your unconscious ways of working will enable you to become even more effective and influential as a leader.

Having two daughters I have become more aware of the fashion industry. When I look back at some of my old photographs I laugh at some of the things I was wearing. Yet at the time they were so cool! I'm sure you have photographs like that too.

The fashion industry have known how to lead for years and work effectively to promote their new fashions on a regular basis. They use people we admire, we want to be like, trust, respect and in some cases love. If the new colour is orange and wearing feathers is in, then we follow. After a while it becomes tribal and you would look wrong if you weren't following the fashion! Successful brands are the same, they develop aspirational brands we all want to be part of. What about your Leadership Brand, do people want to follow you?

By now I'm sure you are wondering what is it that you have to do to be an effective leader in today's world. And no you don't need to wear orange clothes and feathers in your hair!

The next stage of our journey is focussed on exploring the ways of great leadership in today's context. What do they actually do on a day to day basis to achieve success? I have created the 7 Leadership Truths to give clarity to what you need to do to be even more successful.

Let's explore ...

Leadership Truth Number One: Being 100% Authentic

Many years ago after I had just left the Army and joined a Global Organisation I remember going to a lavish conference in a gorgeous hotel. Large stage and lots of provocative stories of success, our new vision, strategies, plans; all exciting stuff. I remember a Sales Director standing up, dressed in his expensive suit, and walking to the stage to give his big motivational speech. He turned, took a big breath and started the presentation with a rallying call, "Our sales are going to grow and grow!"

He had a huge smile and stood very tall. All very positive except for one thing. As he started to speak he had his hands wide apart and as he presented his rallying call to the troops his hands got closer and closer together, the complete opposite to grow and grow.

We work with horses to give leaders the very best feedback they can get. Horses are prey animals so are always on the lookout for danger. They organise themselves to do this and can spot danger from a long way.

We utilise this in-built process to give feedback to see if the leader we are working with is authentic or not. If authentic the horse sees no danger and will work with you. If you are being unauthentic then the horse picks up on this and is wary as you present a real danger to them. Do you know any Managers like that?

With the Sales Director he was being incongruent, unauthentic and it showed. No wonder he didn't have a good reputation in the business and had to lead with fear and coercion. Needless to say his results never came in and we shared him with the competition.

The first truth is around you as a person and for me a key aspect of success in today's world. Today we have to work cross organisationally as well as cross functionally. We are having to work with people who don't report directly to us, people we have no control over. We are having to lead in a different way.

Leadership Truth Number One is about being 100% authentic. It's around understanding who you are and being yourself. It's about self-awareness and playing to your strengths. It's about creating an environment where people trust you as a leader. They get you, they buy into you, they understand where you are coming from and they want to follow and I think what that does is that it comes from being 100% authentic, in horse speak, you are no danger.

One of the key things that I recommend is to really start to build your self-awareness as a leader. Understand who you really are and make sure you are playing to your strengths and you build on your strengths. You need to build a Leadership Brand (I will show you how later.) and be able to talk about your leadership philosophy.

"IN A WORLD OF CONSTANT CHANGE, AMBIGUITY, COMPLEXITY AND UNCERTAINTY FOLLOWERS CAN BE SCARED TOO! IT IS IMPORTANT LEADERS SEE THAT THEIR ROLE IS TO ENSURE PEOPLE FEEL SAFE AND SECURE. ONCE YOU HAVE DONE THAT THEY WILL SURPRISE YOU!"

GRAHAM WILSON

I see so many companies with poor performance management systems destroying confidence and trying to identify what people can't do. What they then do is they send people on training courses to try and correct the things that they'll never be very good at. I disagree with that.

Imagine having a performance conversation with a famous footballer who is the star striker. Most people would call this an appraisal, how outdated and condescending is that. You bring them in to your office and you say to them, "Look you've scored some fantastic goals, you've come back from injury, you've had a great season and it's been fantastic. BUT I noticed that when we are training down on the training pitch and it's your turn in goal, well you are really lousy at being in goal. So what I'd like to do this year is send you on a really expensive goalkeeper's course because I think that's an area of your weakness and we need to improve on that." You just wouldn't do that in sport would you? You'd send them on a goal scoring course on how to score more goals. I think in business we have it the wrong way around. We try and identify what people's weaknesses are and then send them on courses into areas that really they'll never be good at.

My experience of creating high performance in organisations proves it's got to be done the other way around. You have to identify what people's strengths are and then develop those strengths. Sure, be aware of some of your weaknesses and some of the areas you need to compensate for, or areas that you need to bring other people into your team to bolster that particular area, but make sure you are playing to your strengths. The more you play to your strengths, the more authentic you'll be.

I think there is a famous quote from Goffee and Jones in "Why Should Anyone Be Led by You" – They say leadership is all about, "Being more you, with more skill." I think that's really important, it's about playing to your strengths and developing your skills in your strength areas and making sure you use them.

I think another aspect of being 100% authentic is around energy and having the energy to be able to drive change and drive performance in the business. I think resiliency is a really important element in this truth, being resilient and being mindful. I think mindfulness is a huge topic that we need to explore in terms of being in the moment, to being present, really trusting your thoughts and feelings and understanding what's really going on. Not just inside you but the impact you are having on other people so I think being mindful is a key element in today's fast paced world we live in. Go and practice it.

Being healthy and having vitality are all parts of the jigsaw of being authentic. As a leader I think you need to be healthy, you need to understand how to manage high levels of stress and challenge. You need to thrive on a constantly changing environment. So building your health, your strength, your fitness, your flexibility, your resiliency is a key aspect to this first truth. So I know certainly when I am working with a leader who is being authentic, in the moment and vibrant then I am more likely going to follow that leader and trust them.

So, leadership truth number one is all about being an authentic leader that people want to follow.

Two Pots: A perfect tale of perfection!

Many years ago over in China there was a lovely man who lived in a mountain village. Because he loved his beautiful wife and family so much he got up early every morning and he would pick up two pots with one of those sticks you put across your back, and he would walk for a mile and a half to a river to pick up clean water.

This meant his family could get washed and have breakfast. It put a smile on his face seeing them happy. He did this every single morning. He would walk down the same path pick up the water in the pots, turn around, and then come back the same route every single morning. Being a perfectionist and loving order he did this the same way every morning.

However this story is really about the two pots. One day the pots get talking to each other. One of the pots unfortunately had a few cracks in it and the water would leak out of it so by the time the lovely man had got back from the river to home the pot was only a third full. The other pot on the other hand was nice and shiny and brand new and had no cracks in it and didn't leak.

During the conversation the perfect pot said to the cracked pot, "You seem to be a bit down at the moment, what is wrong?" The cracked pot was really upset and given the opportunity poured out his sadness. "I feel really humbled in your presence and admire how perfect you are. Every day we come back and you are still full of water. I'm only a third full if I'm lucky and I feel really upset about that. I feel like I'm broken and not providing as much value as you do."

The perfect pot thought about this for a while and replied, "Well have you ever noticed that on the way down there are some really beautiful flowers on one side of the path, and have you noticed that the man picks some of the flowers for his wife every single morning? He brings the flowers back and he puts them in a vase and his wife comes down to breakfast and sees the flowers and is really happy."

The cracked pot said, "Yes I have noticed this, it makes me feel great seeing the smile on his wife's face every morning. "And have you noticed that the flowers only grow on one side of the path?" asked the perfect pot. "Yes it is strange isn't it?" replied the cracked pot. "Why do you think that is?" asked the perfect pot.

The cracked pot thought about this for a little while and realised that what was obviously happening was that as they were walking back from collecting the water every single day the cracked pot was watering the flowers and making the flowers beautiful. On the other side of the path where the pot was not leaking there was no water and no flowers grew.

I think the secret as a leader is to understand that we all have imperfections and to understand what it is that you do to really add value to your team, to your business, to your family and to your life. When you search hard enough I'm sure you will find that you do add amazing value and you make someone's life really beautiful. It's not about being perfect, it is about being real and authentic.

Speeding up by slowing down - pause for thought!

Now that we have explored the importance of being 100% authentic and having a story to tell it is a good time to connect the learning to you and think about your actions. I will share a Leadership Brand exercise with you in stage 3 so for now have a reflect on whether you are being authentic. The table below will build as we go through the seven truths and will give you areas to think about. The questions below will also get you thinking.

100% Authentic	Inspire Action	High Performance Teams	Innovation	Manage Ambiguity and Kill Risk	Education	Execution
Build self awareness Focus on your strengths Create a Leadership Brand Talk about your Philosophy Be true to yourself Practice vulnerability						

100% Authentic - Leadership actions to think about:

- I work on my three greatest weaknesses and strengths
- My actions reflect my core values
- I openly share my feelings with others
- I do not allow group pressure to control me
- I listen closely to the ideas of others
- I let others know who I truly am as a person and share my leadership philosophy

- I seek feedback as a way of understanding who I really am as a person
- I rarely present a "false" front to others.
- I admit my mistakes to others
- My actions demonstrate that health and wellbeing is important to me and my team

Leadership Truth Number One: Being 100% Authentic

Learn: What have you learnt from this section? Record your thoughts here.

_____

_____

_____

_____

Connect: What does this learning mean to you? Jot down real life situations where you can connect the learning.

_____

_____

_____

_____

Act: What are your specific actions you are going to take to apply your learning?

_____

_____

_____

_____

Leadership Truth Number Two: Inspire Action

When the financial crisis happened I was invited to go to one of the banks to help them really explore great leadership and how we develop great leadership. I needed to help them to understand the challenges they had ahead in terms of developing their leaders. To start the conference I shared a story that I heard many years ago about a company who had invited a world famous pianist to speak at a leadership conference. The idea was to explore the difference between a good musician and a great musician. What makes a great musician and then link this to what makes a great leader.

You can imagine, you've got this famous pianist on the stage, with his grand piano and he's playing some amazing music and you've got a group of business leaders in the room and they are waiting for THE answer. He used an analogy to explain the difference. If you imagine there were six pianists that were about to go onto the stage and play the same instrument, so you could say the piano is the organisation all six leaders work in. They are all also going to play the same music, so you could say the music is the strategy. What is the difference between a good pianist and a great pianist? A good pianist would come up on the stage, play the piano and play it technically correct. All the notes in the right order, the right tempo, all the right nuances, and at the end of the performance because it was perfectly executed the audience would clap and say bravo, that was a great demonstration, well done, fantastic.

And then he shared what a great musician would do. The difference between a good musician and a great musician is that a great musician would do one more thing. They would come on stage and they would play all the notes in the right order, be technically correct, just like the good musician but they would do one more thing.

What they would do is give meaning to the music to the audience. So a great leader is someone who can take a strategy, and can communicate it in a way that gives it meaning to everyone in the organisation in such a way that it inspires action. It inspires people to want to take action after they hear about the strategy.

But strategy isn't enough. In the military if you asked a Brigadier what would they prefer, a great strategy or a Battalion who are really confident and engaged? They would say both. We have to focus on the culture too. It is no good having a great strategy if the culture is no good.

Leadership Truth Number Two is all about the ability of a leader to be able to communicate strategy with meaning and create the right culture . You must have the skills to be able to inspire people to want to take action. It is about your ability to tell stories, encourage constructive dialogue, to use metaphor, to communicate in a way that ensures people are fully engaged, they have emotional commitment to be there and make a difference.

As a leader you are a purpose maximiser, you create a sense of real value, you help people believe that they can make a difference,

You Inspire Action.

Speeding up by slowing down - pause for thought!

Have a think and reflect on your leadership behaviour. Do you communicate your strategies, plans, ideas with meaning.
Do you focus on creating the right culture? At whatever level you are in the organisation this matters. You need to do it as a CEO and you need to do it as a team leader.

100% Authentic	Inspire Action	High Performance Teams	Innovation	Manage Ambiguity and Kill Risk	Education	Execution
Build self awareness Focus on your strengths Create a Leadership Brand Talk about your Philosophy Be true to yourself Practice vulnerability	Communicate with meaning Inspire a common purpose Operate around values Great storyteller Do what is right Why, How and What					

Inspire Action - Leadership actions to think about:

- I inspire a shared purpose
- I role model for belief in and commitment to the organisation
- I focus on how what I do and what others do contributes to the purpose
- I inspire others in tough situations by helping them to focus on the value of their contribution
- I challenge beyond my remit
- I actively promote values and principles

- I take responsibility to put things right outside my remit
- I have the self confidence to challenge others in the face of opposition
- I give examples and stories to communicate my message
- I start with purpose and reasons why before moving into the how and what

Leadership Truth Number Two: Inspire Action

Learn: What have you learnt from this section? Record your thoughts here.

Connect: What does this learning mean to you? Jot down real life situations where you can connect the learning.

Act: What are your specific actions you are going to take to apply your learning?

TEAMWORK

Leadership Truth Three: They create high performance teams

As a leader you achieve your results through the teams around you. In today's world of globalisation, dispersed geographical teams, chaotic projects, and many temporary relationships we need to know how to do teaming. This means getting people together who don't know each other and getting them up to speed quickly so that you can work together effectively. Let me ask you a question. When you put a team together say for a new project what do you focus on first, deliverables or relationships?

If I was to ask the question, which one are you measured on? Would that focus your answer? In my leadership teaching I have asked this question many times, the answer is always deliverables. The danger is of course we get sucked into the deliverables before we have built the team and just expect the team to perform.

Many years ago I was doing a number of teambuilding sessions with a client. They kept sending their teams to us to rescue them. The message we were getting from the client was that the teams started off okay in terms of performance but it had dwindled in the past few months. Tensions were high, relationships breaking down and they were having a tough time trying to hit deliverables.

After a few different teams had left all fired up and ready to rock, it dawned on me that the managers of the teams had no idea how to build teams in the workplace, and that the real problem we needed to sort out was them. I arranged to meet the Director and shared my thinking. He loved the idea as of course it would save him plenty of budget! And I felt ethically great even though I had lost out on plenty of revenue from doing teambuilds for them.

I taught their managers at all levels how to build teams in the workplace. The performance improvement was exponential. For the first time teams had been set up for success. I had taught them how to build and sustain elite teams quickly. What do you do to build and sustain team performance?

When we look at today's world and all the ambiguity and complexity it brings we also need to build alliances, partnerships, global teams, multicultural teams, and virtual teams. All require a high level of skill and process to create effectively and quickly. Many of the commercial opportunities that are out there today require organisations to put a multi-disciplined team together quickly and efficiently. One of the clients I work with in the UK had just added £240M to its top line in 18 months by being the first to grab a change in government policy. They achieved this because they are agile and can form teams quickly. The competition were still going through the planning and risk processes.

If we focus on deliverables and not bother with enabling the team for success we fall foul of the attendees syndrome. This is where you have "attendees" rather than a group of highly engaged and enabled people doing great stuff together. The problem is many leaders rely on a strategy of hope when it comes to building teams. You need to learn how to do it and become a teambuilding wizard! I have a toolkit available to achieve this, check out my website grahamwilson.com

Your job is to set up and develop a team who can move from being managed by you to ultimately being self managed and you adopting a leadership role. Your job is to make yourself redundant. By the way, you can get promoted then. You can't if you are the controlling manager. If I did promote you your team results would crash. Think about that for a while.

Questions for you:
Do you have a team building process you use to set up your teams for success or do you have a strategy of hope? Have you created a situation where you can't be promoted?

Speeding up by slowing down - pause for thought!

What do you do to build your teams, set them up for success and sustain high performance?

100% Authentic	Inspire Action	High Performance Teams	Innovation	Manage Ambiguity and Kill Risk	Education	Execution
Build self awareness Focus on your strengths Create a Leadership Brand Talk about your Philosophy Be true to yourself Practice vulnerability	Communicate with meaning Inspire a common purpose Operate around values Great storyteller Do what is right Why, How and What	Build around a Purpose Build Trust Use a Process Plan together Agree Ways of Working Build Relationships Exploit Technology Build Confidence Empower when team is ready Value People Use Action Learning Celebrate Success				

Create High Performance Teams - Leadership actions to think about:

- I encourage collaboration and actively discourage silo thinking
- I spend time developing my team
- I focus on relationships and building trust
- I hold regular reviews to ensure the team learns and develops
- My team meetings are exciting, challenging and productive
- I ensure team members are playing to strengths
- There is a strong team identity in all my teams

- Clarity of purpose, principles and goals are clear to all team members
- We regularly co-build solutions
- I focus on developing a high performance culture

Leadership Truth Number Three: Build High Performance Teams

Learn: What have you learnt from this section? Record your thoughts here.

Connect: What does this learning mean to you? Jot down real life situations where you can connect the learning.

Act: What are your specific actions you are going to take to apply your learning?

OVERVIEW: THEY CREATE A CULTURE WHERE EVERYONE COMES UP WITH GREAT IDEAS TO IMPROVE PERFORMANCE AND ADD VALUE, THEY INNOVATE IN EVERY ASPECT OF BUSINESS, THEY ARE RELENTLESS DISCOVERERS, THEY EXPLOIT TECHNOLOGY AND PLATFORMS.

Leadership Truth Four: Innovation

We live in a world of accelerating change, of uncertainty, of ambiguity, and volatility. The world is rapidly moving from the knowledge based economy to an innovation economy. The rapid acceleration of the pace of change has caused a situation where we need to constantly innovate in everything we do, or we die! When you look at the businesses who are struggling and failing a common theme that appears is poor leadership and not being agile enough in their ways of working. What this means for us as leaders is that we constantly need to do things in a new and better way.

For me innovation is not just about new products or services it should embrace everything we do. From business modelling, to partnerships and alliances, to processes, products, services, customer journey, brand; in everything we do. It is not just for the R&D teams. We need a new breed of leader who can create a culture where everyone is looking to do things differently, better, faster and cheaper. We need to be focussed on adding more value for our customers and reduce costs – true value innovation. Innovation for me is where we take an idea and turn it into money or value.

In a management hierarchy this is really difficult to do as they operate too slowly and the wrong people make the decisions of what gets approved. The old way of thinking about innovation is as a funnel where ideas are thought of and sent into those "who know", who then decide, based on their views, what gets done. This just doesn't work anymore. It isn't possible that "those who know" at the top of the organisation have had the valuable insight of what needs to be done today.

A new way to look at innovation is to view it as starting with the customer experience and then working backwards to create a solution. You need to think like a designer! The design thinking process is best thought of as a system of overlapping spaces rather than a sequence of orderly steps. There are three spaces to keep in mind: inspiration, ideation, and implementation. I look at it as gaining insight externally by observing and experiencing, generating ideas, building and testing, and then implementing.

Many organisations fall into the trap of sending people on creativity courses as the only solution to improve innovation. They are fun courses by the way, but they don't really help you innovate any better. They help you develop plenty of ideas!! Creativity is the generation of ideas, innovation is the discipline of making money out of them or making them add real value.

Our job as leaders is to create the environment where ideas are freely and constantly generated. You have to create the space for people to be curious, to think, to learn, to create and to implement. You have to create an environment where everyone is striving to be the best they can be and deliver as much value as possible.

Just remember you can always innovate in the area you have control over, your circle of control and influence. You need to create an environment where your team are always looking to be better at what they do. You can innovate around how you run meetings, use technology, organise yourselves, communicate, core processes, solving problems, making decisions, doing projects, form filling, office layout and a whole host of other areas.

A final thought. With the advances in technology we also have to strive to be technologically savvy. There are many solutions out there we have to keep an eye on and up to date with. We need to exploit technology.

Questions for you:
Do you have an innovation process in place? Have you created the culture where curiosity, improvement, ideas, insights and learning are utilised to improve performance?

Speeding up by slowing down - pause for thought!

Have a think and reflect on your leadership behaviour. Have you set up an innovative culture? How do you promote innovation, how do you empower people to take action and make improvement happen? Do your people know how to innovate effectively?

100% Authentic	Inspire Action	High Performance Teams	Innovation	Manage Ambiguity and Kill Risk	Education	Execution
Build self awareness Focus on your strengths Create a Leadership Brand Talk about your Philosophy Be true to yourself Practice vulnerability	Communicate with meaning Inspire a common purpose Operate around values Great storyteller Do what is right Why, How and What	Build around a Purpose Build Trust Use a Process Plan together Agree Ways of Working Build Relationships Exploit Technology Build Confidence Empower when team is ready Value People Use Action Learning Celebrate Success	It is in everything we do Use an innovation process Use tools to generate insights and ideas Clarity in selecting the right ideas Engage stakeholders and the business Removing barriers and kill risks Ensure perfect execution through projects Keep an eye on technology			

Unleash Innovation - Leadership actions to think about:

- I have a clear and communicated innovation process in place for innovation to happen
- I use a variety of tools and techniques to generate new ideas
- I have a clear selection process in place to select the ideas to focus on
- I ensure buy in from the business for new ideas
- I manage stakeholders effectively

- I kill risk early and create effective change plans
- I regularly attend networking events and workshops outside my sector
- I create compelling visions for new ideas
- I prioritise action effectively
- I lead projects effectively to ensure ideas are implemented

Leadership Truth Number Four: Innovation

Learn: What have you learnt from this section? Record your thoughts here.

Connect: What does this learning mean to you? Jot down real life situations where you can connect the learning.

Act: What are your specific actions you are going to take to apply your learning?

Leadership Truth Number Five: Manage Ambiguity and Kill Risk

As you now know one of the many challenges we have as a leader is what we were taught at school. When we were at school there was always THE answer. What that creates is what we call 'OR THINKING.' A classic example of this in business is the question, "Should we be decentralised or centralised?" In hospitals it could be a question like, "Should we be clinically led or commercially led? In sales it could be, "Should we be volume led or margin led."

All these situations are of course paradoxes. If you take the first question, centralised or decentralised then there are pros and cons for both ways. I see many organisations swinging from one to the other. Costs are too high, we are in chaos, we have lost control. We need control, lets centralise everything. So over a two year period everything gets centralised and they move into a phase of our innovation is poor, people are demotivated, we seem to be too far from our customers, let's decentralise.

Of course the answer is that we need 'AND THINKING.' We should build organisations that have the best of centralisation and the best of decentralisation. We need to manage the paradox and reap the rewards. I truly believe that AND THINKING would be a great catalyst for the NHS reforms in the UK. We need a health service that is both clinically AND commercially driven.

Many organisations that call me in for leadership development are so complex it is mind boggling. They don't need to be complex they just seem to want to make it complex! A key aspect of managing ambiguity is to ensure everyone is operating with big picture clarity. To do this we need to get back to basics, kill complexity and remind ourselves what it is that we really do. I love the Business Model Canvas (businessmodelgeneration. com) approach to getting your business onto a page, great for business modelling and managing ambiguity. Get all your strategies and plans on one page. Then communicate them visually and with meaning for all.

The way leaders and organisations manage risk is always an interesting observation. I see plenty of meetings being held with the wrong people in the room, usually senior management, who then have a fight about what the risks are. I always find it interesting how we have this habit of one person having the pen at the flip chart. It is great if they agree with you, they write it down. However if they don't it is fascinating how they turn what you say into written words of what they think, or even worse they don't even write it down. Why can't we all have pens and get the risks down and then debate them?

I remember being shocked at a Board Meeting years ago when someone whispered don't mention that (a big risk) because if you mention it in a Board Meeting it will be logged and we will have to do something about it! Bizarre behaviour don't you think?

For me managing risk is so important. You have to shift into anticipating mode and ask the what if questions. You have to get the right people in the room and identify the risks and then do something about removing them.

The real issue is that we get too busy to spend time anticipating and rush into the delivery mode. We do, however, always find time to put it right when it has gone wrong. What is worse we feel great and pat ourselves on our backs for being the rescuer!

Questions for you:
Do you do OR THINKING or AND THINKING? Do you manage risk proactively or reactively? Do you simplify things?

Speeding up by slowing down - pause for thought!

100% Authentic	Inspire Action	High Performance Teams	Innovation	Manage Ambiguity and Kill Risk	Education	Execution
Build self awareness Focus on your strengths Create a Leadership Brand Talk about your Philosophy Be true to yourself Practice vulnerability	Communicate with meaning Inspire a common purpose Operate around values Great storyteller Do what is right Why, How and What	Build around a Purpose Build Trust Use a Process Plan together Agree Ways of Working Build Relationships Exploit Technology Build Confidence Empower when team is ready Value People Use Action Learning Celebrate Success	It is in everything we do Use an innovation process Use tools to generate insights and ideas Clarity in selecting the right ideas Engage stakeholders and the business Removing barriers and kill risks Ensure perfect execution through projects Keep an eye on technology	Higher Purpose Kill Complexity Use Visual Techniques Kill risk early Use dialogue Work with paradoxes Keep agile and open Keep it Simple Why, What and How		

Manage Ambiguity and Kill Risks - Leadership actions to think about:

- I actively simplify things
- I use one page strategies and plans
- I use visual management techniques
- I can work with paradoxes
- I keep an open and agile mind

- I regularly review and update plans
- I am happy working in an emerging way
- I spending time anticipating the future
- I identify and kill risk immediately
- I use systems thinking to ensure alignment

Leadership Truth Number Five: Manage Ambiguity and Kill Risk

Learn: What have you learnt from this section? Record your thoughts here.

Connect: What does this learning mean to you? Jot down real life situations where you can connect the learning.

Act: What are your specific actions you are going to take to apply your learning?

"THE GROWTH AND DEVELOPMENT OF PEOPLE IS THE HIGHEST CALLING OF LEADERSHIP"

HARVEY S. FIRESTONE

Leadership Truth Number Six: Educate to Inspire

My Grandfather used to work in the docks in Liverpool which, as you can imagine, was a tough environment. When he retired from managing the largest tobacco warehouse in the world and with over 40+ years of experience, I asked him what he had learnt about leadership. His reply was very profound, "When I started leading I thought leadership was about being right and having all the answers. What I learnt is that leadership is all about the ability of asking the right questions to drive the right thinking and action."

Great leaders provide the opportunity for their team to solve the questions themselves. This could include leadership questions, coaching, mentoring or teaching.

Someone once said that the role of a leader is not to create followers but to turn followers into leaders, I agree. Great leaders educate to ensure the capability is in place to achieve outstanding results.

If you took five people with similar backgrounds, similar experience and similar skills and gave them a traditional knowledge and skill training course you would probably expect the same improvement from all five. Research shows that you will get one person who exceeds your expectations, two that match your expectation and two that don't meet expectations yet.

When you think about why one person is exceeding expectations it boils down to one thing, their personal motivation. I believe personal motivation has a vital role to play for leaders.

We can't motivate people but we can create the conditions for people to choose to be motivated. When you look at the amount of training done in organisations the majority of it is around skills and knowledge. They are missing a key element, it should also be about motivation.

Education is not just about knowledge and skills development, it is about motivation development as well. As a thought I just wondered how much motivational development have you done for yourself and for your team this month?

We need to build education, learning, curiosity, courage, questioning, challenging, reviewing and learning into our daily practices.

When my daughters were at school I always used to ask them what they had learnt that day when we were having our family dinner. It became a standing joke and a certain amount of eye rolling during their teenage years, but I wanted to get them into the habit of thinking and learning. We need to do this with our teams at work too.

Team review sessions are a fantastic time to speed up by slowing down. It gives you the opportunity to reflect and acknowledge effort and success and learn from that. A key word often missed from reviews is why. Why were we successful? Why are people feeling like that? Why isn't that process working? Why did that fail? We go into action mode too quickly.

There are a couple of fantastic tools in Stage Four of the book called the action review and journey map. Have a look and use them. You will be amazed at what a difference it makes to your team and your results.

"TRAIN PEOPLE WELL ENOUGH SO THEY CAN LEAVE, TREAT THEM WELL ENOUGH SO THEY DON'T WANT TO."

RICHARD BRANSON

Let's have a look at this motivational element of this leadership truth. Daniel Pink nails motivation for me in his book "Drive". Like Daniel I believe motivation has three vital ingredients that you as a leader must ensure are in place. If any of the three ingredients are missing it is like someone kicking the leg away from the three legged milking stool you are on. Motivation is destroyed and you fall off the stool! It would be like baking a cake with no eggs or flour, it just doesn't work.

So what are the three vital ingredients for motivation?

Do you know a really intelligent person who can't get out of bed in the morning? Someone who is not achieving their potential? The first ingredient is Purpose – understanding why you are doing what you are doing, being on purpose, and understanding what you want to achieve increases motivation. It gives Focus. Imagine a fully charged battery just sitting there. It doesn't do anything until a load is applied. Make sure you apply the load in terms of purpose and goals.

The second element is Attitude. Willingness is a key element for success. This is about ensuring your team have autonomy to act. You need to ensure they have the right attitude and then get out of their way. Attitude is like a muscle, what you exercise gets stronger and bigger. Make sure it is a positive attitude you are exercising.

The final element is Confidence. You achieve this through practice, training, pushing boundaries, getting people out of their comfort zones with support and ensuring people are striving for mastery. You need to create a culture where people want to be their best. There is a great tool in stage four showing you how to do this, see Building Confidence using Mindset Zones.

We talked about the need to build elite teams quickly and to get your team to a level of self-management earlier in the book. You do this by coaching and developing them.

Only if the skill, knowledge and motivation level is low do you use a leadership style of telling and directing. You don't want to get stuck there otherwise you will always be busy and not reap the rewards from the team.

You need to educate, coach, mentor, teach members to increase their skill, knowledge and motivation levels. When they are capable that is when you can back off and support them. This allows you to then take on more leadership activities. You can then lead with questions and nurture talent.

You need to get your team sharing knowledge, teaching each other. Find out what each persons strengths are and get them to share how they do it. I am a big fan of on the job learning. Make sure you work out how you can build elements of learning into daily routines. Be it through review, in your meetings, in workshops, visits to other organisations, or perhaps job swaps. Find out what will work in your situation and make it happen. When people are learning they are growing, they are motivated.

Questions for you:
How much time do you spend developing individuals and the team? Is it enough? Do you have individual and team development plans in place? Do you see review meetings as an opportunity to learn and motivate? Do you nurture and develop capability?

Speeding up by slowing down - pause for thought!

100% Authentic	Inspire Action	High Performance Teams	Innovation	Manage Ambiguity and Kill Risk	Education	Execution
Build self awareness Focus on your strengths Create a Leadership Brand Talk about your Philosophy Be true to yourself Practice vulnerability	Communicate with meaning Inspire a common purpose Operate around values Great storyteller Do what is right Why, How and What	Build around a Purpose Build Trust Use a Process Plan together Agree Ways of Working Build Relationships Exploit Technology Build Confidence Empower when team is ready Value People Use Action Learning Celebrate Success	It is in everything we do Use an innovation process Use tools to generate insights and ideas Clarity in selecting the right ideas Engage stakeholders and the business Removing barriers and kill risks Ensure perfect execution through projects Keep an eye on technology	Higher Purpose Kill Complexity Use Visual Techniques Kill risk early Use dialogue Work with paradoxes Keep agile and open Keep it Simple Why, What and How	Regular Review Ask Why Learn from Success and Failure Coach Teach Stretch Rotate Jobs Get people out of their comfort zone Focus on Skill Knowledge and Motivation	

Education - Leadership actions to think about:

- I use and encourage action learning techniques
- I build in learning reviews as a way of working
- I review feelings, behaviours, and methods as well as outcomes
- I regularly challenge and ask why questions to promote learning
- I actively coach my team members
- I encourage informal on the job learning
- I develop the confidence of my team
- I encourage curiosity and lead with questions
- I ensure my team get outside their normal environment to learn
- I focus on learning from success and failure

Leadership Truth Number Six: Educate to Inspire

Learn: What have you learnt from this section? Record your thoughts here.

Connect: What does this learning mean to you? Jot down real life situations where you can connect the learning.

Act: What are your specific actions you are going to take to apply your learning?

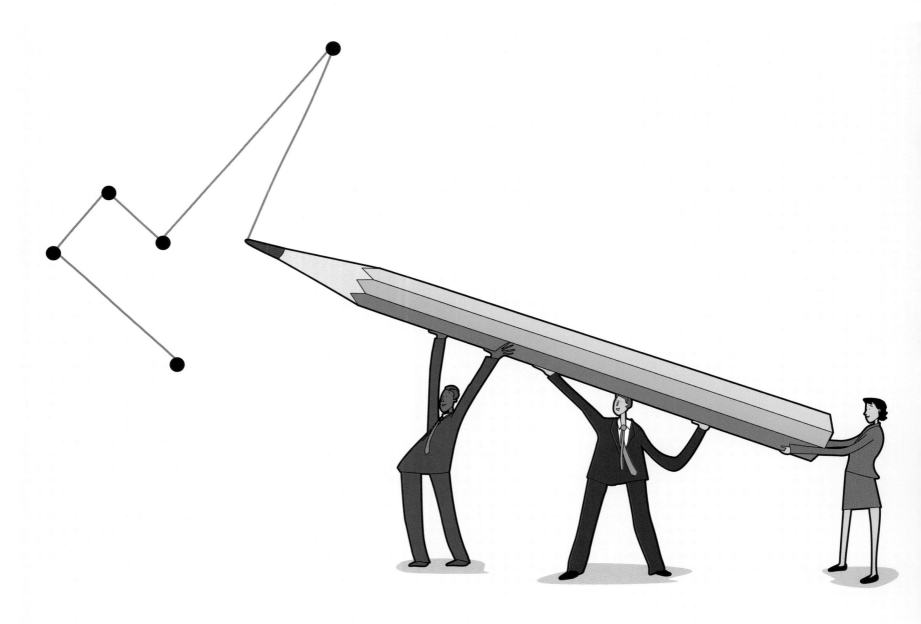

Leadership Truth Number Seven: Execute with Pace

There is a Japanese proverb that says, "A vision without action is a dream." As a leader it is important to know your purpose. You also have to know how to execute with pace, otherwise you add no value. This is where all the other six truths manifest themselves. You have to use all the skills you have used implementing these truths and focus them on delivery with pace. This is about your personal productivity and your ability to influence and persuade.

Simon Sinek tells a wonderful story of how Steve Jobs and some of his senior executives went to Xerox, PARC in the early 1980s and were shown something that Xerox had developed called the graphic user interface. The problem was, Steve Jobs, with his vision of seamlessly integrating technology into our lives, sees this graphic user interface and sees it as a much better way to getting to his vision. So, he says to his executives, "We have to invest in this graphic user interface thing." And his executives say to him, "Steve, if we invest in this, we're gonna blow up our own business." To which he replies, "Better we should blow it up than someone else." And that decision became the Macintosh.

Remember the three leadership principles of Boldness, Simplicity and Speed we talked about earlier. This is a clear demonstration of these by Steve Jobs. Having the willingness to take the bold decisions, follow your dream and make it happen is vital to your success. Simplicity of execution is key here, you as a leader need to operate around four key elements. Your purpose (the Why), your goals (the What) and the plan (the How). And all of this has to align to your values (the Way). It is so easy to miss some of the elements and jump into delivery of task. Make sure that everyone on the team knows the why, the what, the how and the way. Keep it simple and make all your decisions around these four elements.

With clarity in place and a team of skilled operators you can manage by exception. This gives you time to do the leadership stuff rather than be bogged down in routine management fire fighting. You can get out of their way and let them perform! You can start to operate and set up personal routines that enable you to take control rather than be controlled by emails and crisis. What do you do daily to set yourself up for success?

Setting up the team, spending a bit more time up front, will enable you to operate with pace. Without this time to ensure clarity and buy in you will be struggling to operate at the speed you need to. I get asked to rescue many project teams who are struggling with delivery. I start by asking them individually a series of questions: Tell me what the purpose of the project is? Why are you doing it? What benefits are you trying to achieve? How does it align to the strategy? Who is on the team? What is their role and what motivates/demotivates them? What are your goals? What are your team values? How are you going to achieve success? What do you want to be famous for? In a high performance team focussed on delivering with pace I would expect all the team members to know the answers. Sadly when I ask the team who are struggling there are massive gaps of knowledge missing. The reason the answers are missing by the way is because the team were led straight into delivery without being set up for success. What I then do is to work through a process to put the project on a page and achieve absolute clarity in all the areas mentioned – your job as a leader is to join the dots and set up your team for success. You can find tools in stage four - Team Playbook and Plan on a Page.

Another key element of delivering with speed is the quality of the reviews held by leaders. It is important to have regular learning reviews to keep on track. It is a great way to celebrate success, ensure clarity, reward people, give recognition and to stimulate learning and continuous improvement.

Speeding up by slowing down - pause for thought!

Have a think and reflect on your leadership behaviour. Do you execute with pace? Are you mainly proactive or are you totally reactive and driven by your email inbox? Do you set yourself and your team up for success everyday? Do your daily routines and habits help or hinder?

100% Authentic	Inspire Action	High Performance Teams	Innovation	Manage Ambiguity and Kill Risk	Education	Execution
Build self awareness Focus on your strengths Create a Leadership Brand Talk about your Philosophy Be true to yourself Practice vulnerability	Communicate with meaning Inspire a common purpose Operate around values Great storyteller Do what is right Why, How and What	Build around a Purpose Build Trust Use a Process Plan together Agree Ways of Working Build Relationships Exploit Technology Build Confidence Empower when team is ready Value People Use Action Learning Celebrate Success	It is in everything we do Use an innovation process Use tools to generate insights and ideas Clarity in selecting the right ideas Engage stakeholders and the business Removing barriers and kill risks Ensure perfect execution through projects Keep an eye on technology	Higher Purpose Kill Complexity Use Visual Techniques Kill risk early Use dialogue Work with paradoxes Keep agile and open Keep it Simple Why, What and How	Regular Review Ask Why Learn from Success and Failure Coach Teach Stretch Rotate Jobs Get people out of their comfort zone Focus on Skill Knowledge and Motivation	Start with Why Give meaning to plans Inspire Action Join the Dots Speed up and Slow Down Deliver through People Execute with Pace Celebrate Make it Fun Keep on Purpose Measure and manage the right things Flex leadership style according to the situation

Execute with pace - Leadership actions to think about:

- I translate strategy to action by giving meaning
- I start with explaining why first rather than what we need to do first
- I hold people accountable
- I ensure people are engaged and enabled
- I regularly review and develop actions
- I praise contribution and outcomes
- I modify my leadership behaviour depending on the situation
- I energise teams
- I create a sense of urgency
- I reward success

Leadership Truth Number Seven: Execute with Pace

Learn: What have you learnt from this section? Record your thoughts here.

Connect: What does this learning mean to you? Jot down real life situations where you can connect the learning.

Act: What are your specific actions you are going to take to apply your learning?

LEADERSHIP LAID BARE

THE NAKED TRUTH OF WHAT GREAT LEADERS ACTUALLY DO

"THEY CREATE A HIGH PERFORMANCE ENVIRONMENT WHERE SUCCESS IS INEVITABLE"

1 LEADERSHIP PURPOSE:
THEY AWAKEN POSSIBILITY IN PEOPLE TO DELIVER EXTRAORDINARY RESULTS

3 LEADERSHIP PRINCIPLES:
THEY OPERATE WITH BOLDNESS, SIMPLICITY AND SPEED

7 LEADERSHIP TRUTHS:
THEY LIVE THE 7 TIMELESS LEADERSHIP PRINCIPLES

1 THEY UNDERSTAND THEMSELVES AND HAVE A STORY TO TELL:
THEY HAVE AN AUTHENTIC LEADERSHIP BRAND, THEY BUILD ON STRENGTHS, THEY ARE HAPPY BEING VULNERABLE, THEY ARE THEMSELVES, THEY SHARE THEIR LEADERSHIP PHILOSOPHY, THEY BUILD TRUST, THEY ARE POSITIVE, HEALTHY AND HAPPY.

2 THEY INSPIRE ACTION:
PURPOSE IS AT THE HEART OF EVERYTHING THEY DO, THEY MAKE A DIFFERENCE, THEY HAVE COURAGE, THEY GO OUT ON A LIMB, THEY ARE BOLD, THEY TELL STORIES AND GIVE EXAMPLES THAT GIVE MEANING AND INSPIRE ACTION. THEY CREATE A SENSE OF REAL VALUE.

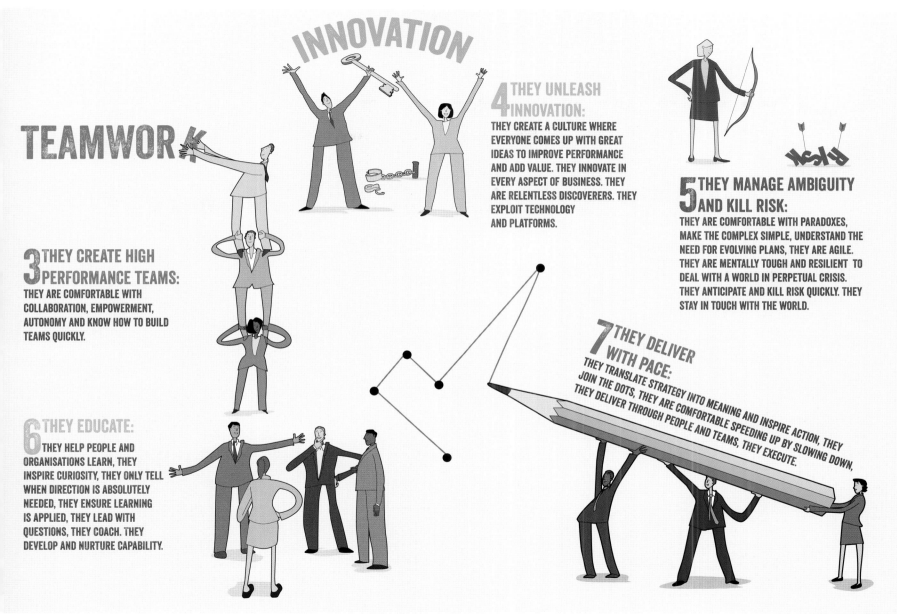

INNOVATION

TEAMWORK

4 THEY UNLEASH INNOVATION:
THEY CREATE A CULTURE WHERE EVERYONE COMES UP WITH GREAT IDEAS TO IMPROVE PERFORMANCE AND ADD VALUE. THEY INNOVATE IN EVERY ASPECT OF BUSINESS. THEY ARE RELENTLESS DISCOVERERS. THEY EXPLOIT TECHNOLOGY AND PLATFORMS.

5 THEY MANAGE AMBIGUITY AND KILL RISK:
THEY ARE COMFORTABLE WITH PARADOXES, MAKE THE COMPLEX SIMPLE, UNDERSTAND THE NEED FOR EVOLVING PLANS, THEY ARE AGILE. THEY ARE MENTALLY TOUGH AND RESILIENT TO DEAL WITH A WORLD IN PERPETUAL CRISIS. THEY ANTICIPATE AND KILL RISK QUICKLY. THEY STAY IN TOUCH WITH THE WORLD.

3 THEY CREATE HIGH PERFORMANCE TEAMS:
THEY ARE COMFORTABLE WITH COLLABORATION, EMPOWERMENT, AUTONOMY AND KNOW HOW TO BUILD TEAMS QUICKLY.

7 THEY DELIVER WITH PACE:
THEY TRANSLATE STRATEGY INTO MEANING AND INSPIRE ACTION, THEY JOIN THE DOTS, THEY ARE COMFORTABLE SPEEDING UP BY SLOWING DOWN, THEY DELIVER THROUGH PEOPLE AND TEAMS, THEY EXECUTE.

6 THEY EDUCATE:
THEY HELP PEOPLE AND ORGANISATIONS LEARN, THEY INSPIRE CURIOSITY, THEY ONLY TELL WHEN DIRECTION IS ABSOLUTELY NEEDED, THEY ENSURE LEARNING IS APPLIED, THEY LEAD WITH QUESTIONS, THEY COACH. THEY DEVELOP AND NURTURE CAPABILITY.

"THE LEARNING IS IN THE WOBBLES."

DAVE MEIER

Summarise key learning points

Now is a good time to consolidate your learning. Take all your learning from stage 1 and stage 2 and record it here.

Killer Mindsets: Role: Purpose: Principles: The 7 Truths

My key insights and learning I can use to improve myself as a leader are:

STAGE 3: WHAT

What to do to improve your leadership capability

Now we have consolidated our learning it is time to take massive action. We have explored what could be stopping us and the need to lead in a different way. You need to unleash yourself from out dated ways of working and develop your way of leading. Now is the time to reclaim your personal power and freedom.

What to do to improve your leadership capability

I have always avoided playing golf. For some reason it just doesn't appeal to me. I much prefer the rough and tumble of team sports. In my role of developing leaders it got to the point where I was being asked too often to play golf to avoid playing. All those charity and corporate events - you get the picture. Not being competitive at all I decided I needed to learn quickly how to play so I could win! I duly booked into a local golf club with the local professional who I had been told was the best in my area. Fantastic I thought.

I duly turned up, and as I was wearing all the wrong gear, we decided to start my lessons on the driving range. Clearly I wasn't dressed right to go on the course. Graham, "See that red flag right in front of you, it is 275 yards away. I want you to take a seven iron and hit the ball as close to the flag as possible."

I thought what is a seven iron? Luckily I spotted the numbers stamped into the clubs. I took my seven iron and decided to be Rory McIlroy. I wiggled my bum a bit and hit the ball. To my amazement it went straight towards the red flag and finished rolling about 15 yards away. Cool I thought!

Feeling proud of myself my coach said, "Now let me show you how to hit a ball and play golf." No well done, just let me tell you. He went on to tell me everything about grip, approaching the ball, my foot positioning, knees, hips, swing, the lot. I then spent the rest of the lesson not being able to hit a ball.

Moral of the story is to take one step at a time. In elite teams and elite sport they regularly talk about making a 1% difference.

We shouldn't try to change everything about how we lead in one go. That would be a disaster like my golf. We need to take a step by step approach. As Dave Brailsford from Sky says, "Go for marginal gains."

To start off with I recommend a four stage process to get the most from this handbook.

Reclaiming your power by building your leadership capability

1: CREATING AND MANAGING YOUR LEADERSHIP BRAND

4: CRAFTING SOLUTIONS

CONTINUALLY IMPROVING

2: LIVING THE NEW LEADERSHIP MANIFESTO

3: BUILDING AND USING YOUR LEADERSHIP TOOLKIT

STEP 1: CREATING AND MANAGING YOUR LEADERSHIP BRAND

You need to know what you stand for as a leader and who you are, and so do the people around you. Your leadership brand helps this. It is important to remember it is a journey - it evolves. It helps you to achieve clarity and supports your decision making. Here are some examples:

DENISE MORRISON,
CEO OF CAMPBELL SOUP COMPANY

"To serve as a leader, live a balanced life, and apply ethical principles to make a significant difference." Morrison said, "The personal mission statement was important for me because I believe that you can't lead others unless you have a strong sense of who you are and what you stand for. For me, living a balanced life means nurturing the academic, physical, and spiritual aspects of my life so I can maintain a sense of well-being and self-esteem."

GRAHAM WILSON,
FOUNDER OF SUCCESSFACTORY™

"Awakening possibility in leaders to deliver extraordinary results".

SIR RICHARD BRANSON,
FOUNDER OF THE VIRGIN GROUP

"To have fun in my journey through life and learn from my mistakes." Branson shared his personal mission statement in an interview with Motivated magazine. He added that "In business, know how to be a good leader and always try to bring out the best in people. It's very simple: listen to them, trust in them, believe in them, respect them, and let them have a go!"

AMANDA STEINBERG,
FOUNDER OF DAILYWORTH.COM

"To use my gifts of intelligence, charisma, and serial optimism to cultivate the self-worth and net-worth of women around the world."

YOURS?

How to create your leadership brand

Your leadership brand is your reputation, it is the promise you make to the people you serve. It helps you to communicate your strengths and what you bring to the world. It is unique to you. The three key areas to think about are:

Authentic: We have already talked about the importance of being you, and being real in the 7 Truths. Your brand has to represent your strengths, the REAL you, and with no hype or spin.

Interesting: It needs to make you stand out and be unique and it needs to stick.

Sticky: It needs to be memorable for the right reasons.

Branding is a journey, not a destination. It involves a four step process and big questions that you'll revisit through your journey.

1. **Discovery :** What are your strengths, values, beliefs?

2. **Focus :** What do you want to be famous for?

3. **Communicate :** What is your message? How are you going to communicate it?

4. **Align :** Are you aligned? Take massive action to align and review regularly. Make sure you are living your brand and are in alignment.

The exercise on the next page will guide you through this process. **The exercise on the next page will guide you through this process.**

"YOUR BRAND IS WHAT PEOPLE SAY ABOUT YOU WHEN YOU ARE NOT IN THE ROOM."

JEFF BEZOS

Blueprinting exercise for building your leadership brand

Your answers

STAGE 1 DISCOVERY **What was your best day at work in the last three months?** What were you doing? Why did you love it? How can we repeat it?	
What was your worst day at work in the last three months? What were you doing? Why did it drain you? How can we avoid it?	
What is the best manager relationship you've ever had? What made it so good?	
What's the best recognition you've ever had? What made it so good?	
When in your career have you learnt most? Why? What was happening? How were you learning?	
What are your values and beliefs? What is important to you?	
Your friends and colleagues thoughts Once you have done this ask your friends and colleagues what they think your strengths are.	
STAGE 2: FOCUS **What do you want to be famous for?** Summarise your answers above, what are the patterns, themes?	
STAGE 3: COMMUNICATE **Create your leadership brand statement** "I want to be known for being _____, and _____ so that I can deliver_____"	
STAGE 4: ALIGN **Take massive action:** What are you going to stop, start and continue doing to live your brand?	

STEP 2: THE LEADERSHIP MANIFESTO
Make a commitment to living the leadership manifesto.

LIVING THE LEADERSHIP MANIFESTO

I ....do solemnly swear to:

Create a high performance environment where success is inevitable.
I will awaken possibility in people to deliver extraordinary results.

I will:
- Be 100% authentic
- Inspire action
- Build an elite team
- Unleash innovation
- Educate and develop to build confidence
- Manage ambiguity and kill risk
- Deliver with pace

Signed ....Date.........................

Step 2: Living the Leadership Manifesto

Greatness has been described by having four key elements in play: being of service, having a clear vision, operating courage and basing action on reality. Make sure these are amplified and they will serve you well in increasing your success.

To live the manifesto you need to see your role of a leader and the purpose of leadership as a commitment. When you go to bed at night ask yourself am I creating a high performance environment where success is inevitable? And how many people did I awaken possibility in today? Am I operating with boldness, simplicity and speed? If not do something about it.

Here are a few great tips to help you live the three principles of Boldness, Simplicity and Speed

5 Ways to Being Bold
1. Focus on your purpose
2. Make a conscious effort to focus on developing your confidence by getting out of your comfort zone regularly
3. Let go of perfection
4. Be inspired by other great people
5. Do something that scares you at least once a year

3 Ways to Ensure Simplicity
1. Keep your Purpose, Vision, Goals, Values in mind and execute around them
2. Sticky Steps Planning - Begin with the end in mind. Ask two questions and use post it notes to plan everything. Use the sayings: In order to ... I must have (Tool in stage four)
3. Ensure clarity with regular review – learn how to review, learn and take action

2 ways to ensure Speed
1. When you need work done always start with WHY, then clarify the WHAT you want to achieve and then let the team work out the HOW, ensuring it is aligned to the WAY
2. Build the team first. Build trust, clarity and relationships first then put the foot on the accelerator to achieve the results you need

STEP 3: BUILDING AND USING YOUR LEADERSHIP TOOLKIT

We are all on a continuing journey of leadership mastery. You have a clear framework to work from so you can start to build your toolkit around the framework. A good starting point is to add what tools you already use to the toolkit I have created for you below. A point to remember is that you will find some tools can be used in more than one area.

Once you have done that it is time to learn the tools I have shared if you haven't used them before. On my face to face masterclass and mastermind sessions I use many of the powerful leadership tools to solve real in the moment leadership challenges.

Many more tools will become available at grahamwilson.com My vision is to create a mini video of each tool showing you how you can use them and available for mobile use.

There are many hundreds of tools so it will take time but the Leadership Vault is building quickly. It would be great to get videos of you using the tools too. Here is a sample Leadership Toolkit mapped against the 7 Truths (please bear in mind that this is a sample of tools and that they are interchangeable and can be used for more than one truth.)

Example Leadership Toolkit shared in Stage 4

100% Authentic	Inspire Action	Build Elite Teams	Unleash Innovation	Manage Ambiguity and Kill Risk	Educate	Execute with Pace
Identifying your Strengths	Golden Circle	Team Vitality	Disney Technique	Dilemmas	Leader Manager	Project Framework
Mad Sad Glad	Plan on a Page	Team Playbook	Radiant Problem	Alignment	Coach	Meetings
Vitality	Visionit	TEAMFLOWS	Solving	Risk Management	PAC Factor	Storyboarding
Trust Formula			World Cafe		Action Review	DIRECT Goal Setting
Circle of Influence					Learning Cycle	DRIVERS (CAP)
					Building Confidence through Mindsets	Coaching Change
						Challenge Support
						Change Bridge
						Journey Map
						Ease Impact Grid
						Leadership Styles

STEP 4: CRAFTING SOLUTIONS USING YOUR LEADERSHIP TOOLKIT

I always remember my early military education, mainly because it was consequential as my life depended on it. One of the many principles that stuck in my mind was that your plan is always useless because when you come in contact with the enemy you have no idea what is going to happen. Your plan will become rapidly redundant.

We were trained in managing these 'dislocated expectations' through having the right open and agile mindset, focussing on the process of the solution, and empowering people to make decisions on the ground. As a leader you ensure the 'why' is in place and then enable success.

This thinking has evolved to my present day approach where I am completely convinced that as a leader we need to craft solutions.

Crafting in my mind evokes a whole new image compared to the tradition, "we must have a detailed plan and 'stick to it' thinking." Crafting is about thinking and doing skills, emotion, mastery, dedication, collaboration, pride, greatness and being your best. When you master this way of 'thinking and doing' you will be amazed at your results.

Crafting in a leadership context is where you design a process using a range of tools along the way to solve a problem or grab an opportunity before starting to tackle it. In a way it helps you to speed up by slowing down. You then implement your process making changes every step of the way as the information unfolds .

The best way to learn this is to do it for real, so let me share a few examples so that you can then take one of your challenges and have a go.

Let's say I'm a Project Manager and I need to get more buy-in for my project and gain more funding to make it happen.

How might I approach this? I could just get busy and hold lots of meetings and try and influence people, and then tell them again, and then again being a little louder and slower - or I could use a crafted solution.

Worked Examples

To craft solutions I recommend using post it notes to aid your thinking. In essence you take your issue, problem, opportunity and you start with the outcomes and work backwards. Then record all the ideas that come up, one idea per post it note. Depending on the situation and context this can be done by yourself or better still with a team. In most cases it is best done with other people as they will add greater insight.

Once you have all the ideas down and identified all the tools you can use, you can create a process. Here are some real life examples. All the tools mentioned are in stage 4 later in the book.

The examples are at the stage where the ideas have been generated on post it notes and then put in order to create the process.

Example 1: In order to: engage the Board in my idea and secure more funding to implement the changes I need for my project
I must:

1. Sell idea of a meeting to Board - use DRIVERS(CAP) Tool to formulate board paper and show what is missing and consequences
2. Have meeting with Board and build a business case by asking what are the implications of not doing it and the benefits of doing it? Show how the idea fits to the strategy Determine blockers and brainstorm solutions using Radiant Problem Solving
3. Build action plan - Use Game Plan Tool to create plan

Example 2: To: solve this issue
I must:

1. Stop and carry out situational analysis - map back to organisational strategy to ensure it needs solving
2. Gain insights internally and externally - ask who has solved this before
3. Generate ideas to solve problem - use Disney Technique and Radiant Problem Solving
4. Classify ideas and select ones to go through - use Ease Impact Grid
5. Gain emotional commitment from business - use DRIVERS(CAP)
6. Making it possible by creating change plan
7. Create a project plan - use Game Plan Tool
8. Keep in track using regular review - Action Review Tool

Example 3: To: set up my project team for success
I must:

1. Clarify Purpose - link team purpose to organisational strategy - Golden Circle
2. Build trust and get to know each other - career journey exercise and use behavioural profiling to understand strengths and values
3. Create team playbook during offsite workshop
4. Create team plan - use Game Plan Tool
5. Select right leadership style - Leadership Styles
6. Keep performance sustained - Review progress once a month with Journey Map and Action Review tools

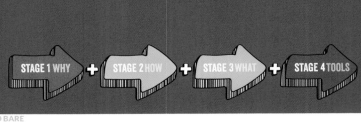

STAGE 4: ACTION

Your Leadership Toolkit

I have included a number of leadership tools that I have discovered over the years and have found useful to craft leadership solutions. These are not all my own tools. I have just collated them into an easy to use format for you to use. They are attributed where possible and I suggest you gain further information from the source. There are many more tools out there - keep searching, applying and learning.

"SOME PEOPLE LIVE LIFE WITHOUT USING ALL THAT THEY HAVE. IT WOULD BE LIKE BUYING AN ASTON MARTIN AND NEVER TAKING IT OUT OF FIRST GEAR!"

GRAHAM WILSON

CONTENTS OF TOOL SECTION

This section contains a number of tools you can use when appropriate. You can dip into them when required. Using the crafting solutions philosophy you can select the right tools to achieve the outcomes you desire. For ease of use I have categorised the tools under each of the leadership truths. Please bear in mind many of the tools can be used in different areas.

Leadership Truth 1 - 100% Authentic
Identifying your Strengths
Mad Sad Glad
Vitality
Trust Formula
Circle of Influence

Leadership Truth 2 - Inspire Action
Golden Circle
Game Plan
Visionit

Leadership Truth 3 - Build Elite Teams
Team Vitality
Team Playbook
TEAMFLOWS

Leadership Truth 4 - Unleash Innovation
Disney Technique
Radiant Problem Solving
World Café

Leadership Truth 5 - Manage Ambiguity and Kill Risk
Alignment
Risk Management
Dilemmas

Leadership Truth 6 - Educate
Leader Manager Coach
PAC Factor
Action Review
Learning Cycle
Building Confidence through Mindsets

Leadership Truth 7 - Execute with Pace
Project Framework
Meetings
Storyboarding
DIRECT Goal Setting
DRIVERS (CAP)
Coaching through Change
Challenge Support
Change Bridge
Journey Map
Ease Impact Grid
Leadership Styles

"AUTHENTICITY IS A COLLECTION OF CHOICES THAT WE HAVE TO MAKE EVERY DAY. IT'S ABOUT THE CHOICE TO SHOW UP AND BE REAL. THE CHOICE TO BE HONEST. THE CHOICE TO LET OUR TRUE SELVES BE SEEN."

BRENÉ BROWN

LEADERSHIP TRUTH 1 - 100% AUTHENTIC

IDENTIFY YOUR STRENGTHS – FIVE QUESTIONS

There is overwhelming evidence that emotional intelligence is one of the biggest drivers of leadership success. Self awareness is the foundation of effective emotional intelligence as this can lead to being more authentic.

1.
What was your best day at work in the last three months?

What were you doing?
Why did you love it?
How can you repeat it?

2.
What was your worst day at work in the last three months?

What were you doing?
Why did it drain you?
How can you avoid it?

3.
What is the best manager relationship you've ever had?

What made it so good?

4.
What's the best recognition you've ever had?

What made it so good?

5.
When in your career have you learnt most?

What was happening?
How were you learning?

IDENTIFY YOUR STRENGTHS – FIVE QUESTIONS

What is it?

A strength is an activity that makes a person feel strong. It's an activity that strengthens them. This tool helps you find out what invigorates your team, what demotivates them and where their aspirations lie. This information is really valuable and will help you identify the areas to enhance their performance.

The five questions are designed to be used in coaching sessions or team review sessions to ensure strengths are being used.

Where can I use it?

- Coaching.
- Team reviews.
- Performance management.
- Informal conversations.

How do I use it?

1. Create a safe and trusting climate.
2. Ask the five questions and listen.
3. Explore the answers and question more to expand.
4. Create actions.
5. Carry out ongoing support and review often.

MAD SAD GLAD

Creating a positive team climate by understanding and valuing difference

	Austin	Susan	Tam	Roberto
What makes you MAD	Avoidable surprises. Problem stating inaccurate/ incomplete data. Not going extra mile for our customers. Not caring about losing good people.	Surprises. Missing deadline requests without explanation. Being missed out of the loop. Having agreed to plan then not completing. Only getting part of the information.	Digressing. People spending too much time on themselves. Lack of structure at meetings. Lack of 1:1 time. Lack of trust in my ability. Lack of direction. Given tasks that aren't followed up.	Being excluded when I could help. Deadlines being missed. Not being responded to. Surprises. Not doing what was agreed or re-negotiating. Festering in the negativity.
What makes you SAD	People who don't care. Working too hard + long hours. Spending lots of time on under-performers instead of high performers.	Doing things the same. Missing opportunities. Missing deadlines. Missed expectations Dissatisfaction over "trivia". Complaints.	Lack of time. Lack of time to 'develop' team. Lack of 'Open Forum' time. Lack of social aspects. Work/Life Balance.	Not being used as support. Not being consulted. Things not working well. Irritating people when it's not my intention. If team didn't see benefits of what striving to achieve.
What makes you GLAD	Manage my expectation and keep me informed. Ask me to make decisions having all info and facts. Create a plan, do + get results. Using initiative. A good debate + dialogue. Having a laugh.	Achieving deadlines. Seeing teams develop. Compliments. Getting external recognition. Getting internal recognition. Being the best. Problem solving not stating. Being creative.	Support. Reassurance. Advice/Guidance. Friendship. Using different strengths. Knowledge base. Positive, enthusiastic caring people.	Getting together + agreeing way forward. Working together to solve challenges. Making a difference. Having fun. Recognition.

Based on work by Manfred Kets de Vries, INSEAD

MAD SAD GLAD

What is it?

A useful tool to help you understand team members . It also guides you in how you communicate with each other and interact in the best way to achieve a positive team climate.

Where can I use it?

Areas it can be used are:
- Building trust
- Building awareness
- Project set up workshops
- Reviewing
- Understand why people are behaving like they are
- Creating a positive work environment
- Team building

How do I use it?

1. Invite team members to a workshop sharing the purpose of the session.
2. Ask each person to think about what makes them Mad, Sad, Glad. Explain why this is useful and what the benefits are of doing it and what it can overcome. Use real life examples to illustrate if possible.
3. Ask each person to think about what makes them Mad, Sad, Glad.
4. Record on table.
5. Use on a regular basis as a review tool to ensure you are working well together.

VITALITY

Keeping strong and healthy as a leader in today's tough world is vital. Here is a simple framework to ensure you get balance in all four areas to increase your vitality.

MOVEMENT

DIET

VITALITY

QUIET

SLEEP

VITALITY

What is it?

- A framework that indicates the key elements required to ensure health and welbeing

Where can I use it?

- Leadership Development.
- Development of new individuals in the team.
- Personal Development

How do I use it?

1. Diet: Make sure you eat a healthy diet full of natural goodies.

2. Sleep: Make sure you get a good sleep everyday. This is your recovery and rebuild time.

3. Quiet: Spend time thinking, meditating, being mindful. I love getting outdoors for a walk and just being .

4. Movement: Ensure you exercise each day. Find something you love and mix it up a bit. Try different exercises on a regular basis.

BUILDING TRUST

Empathy + Reliability + Alignment + Results + Consistency + Brand = Trusted Leader

	What are you going to STOP doing?	What are you going to START doing?	What are you going to CONTINUE?
Empathy (High emotional intelligence, you listen and understand others)			
Reliability (You can be relied upon to do what you promise)			
Alignment (You behave and make decisions aligned to the vision and strategy)			
Results (You deliver the results promised)			
Consistency (You operate consistency to agreed values)			
Brand (You have a clear and articulated leadership brand)			

BUILDING TRUST

What is it?

• A tool for building trust.

Where can I use it?

• Generating actions to improve leadership trust.
• For ongoing personal/team reflection of actions.
• Team sessions for developing a high trust environment.

How do I use it?

• Review and think about each element to develop actions you must stop doing, start doing and continue doing for each element.

CIRCLE OF INFLUENCE

Creating a positive team climate by understanding and valuing difference

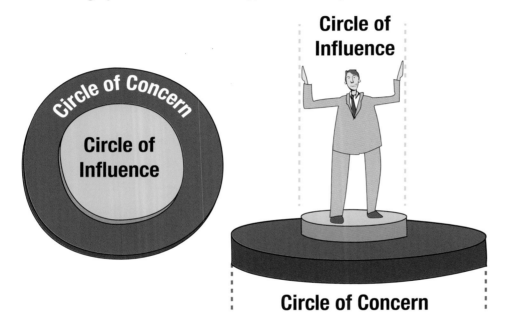

Circle of Concern

Circle of Influence

Circle of Influence

Circle of Concern

Circle of Influence Shrinks

Focussing on things which are outside your control. Focussing on things which you can do nothing about.

Circle of Influence

Circle of Concern

Circle of Influence Grows

Focussing on things which you can influence. Focussing on things which you can do something about, even if it's just focussing on how you react to something in a positive way.

Based on work by Stephen Covey and 7 Habits of Highly Effective People - one of my favourite books!

CIRCLE OF INFLUENCE

What is it?

• A model developed by Stephen Covey to ensure the right thinking is in place for success

Where can I use it?

• Personal development.
• Review sessions.

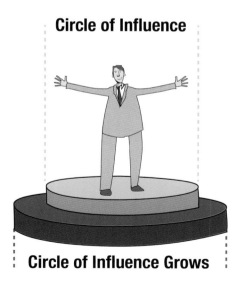

Circle of Influence

Circle of Influence Grows

How do I use it?

1. Review an agreed period of time (e.g. the last 6 months) and ask yourself: Where would I plot the things I have been doing? Have I been: Focussing on things which I can influence? Focussing on things which I can do something about, even if it's just focussing on how I react to something in a positive way?

Or

Focussing on things which are outside my control? Focussing on things which I can do nothing about?

2. Based on the review, what are you going to start doing, stop doing, continue doing to increase your circle of influence?

Note: This is a really helpful tool to help if you are feeling frustrated - it can help you focus on situations where you can influence rather than where you can't (source of frustration).

"THERE ARE ONLY TWO WAYS TO INFLUENCE HUMAN BEHAVIOUR: YOU CAN MANIPULATE IT OR YOU CAN INSPIRE IT."

SIMON SINEK

LEADERSHIP TRUTH 2 - INSPIRE ACTION

THE GOLDEN CIRCLE

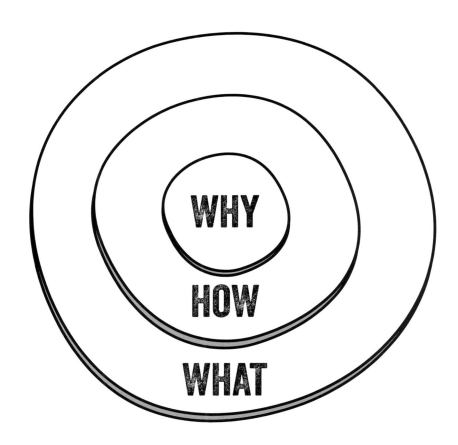

Simon Sinek

THE GOLDEN CIRCLE

What is it?

Developed by Simon Sinek this model codifies the three distinct and interdependent elements (Why, How, What) that makes any person or organisation function at its highest ability. Based on the biology of human decision making, it demonstrates how the function of our limbic brain and the neocortex directly relate to the way in which people interact with each other and with organisations and brands in the formation of cultures and communities.

Where can I use it?

- Inspiring action
- Creating strategy
- Communicating to engage
- Objective setting
- To summarise a 6P's workshop
- Planning

How do I use it?

Whether you are looking to create a change strategy, influence people, inspire action or communicate to engage it is important to start with WHY. Once you have developed the WHY then communicate HOW and then the WHAT.

Following this sequence will improve understanding and inspire action.

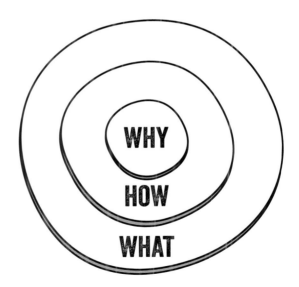

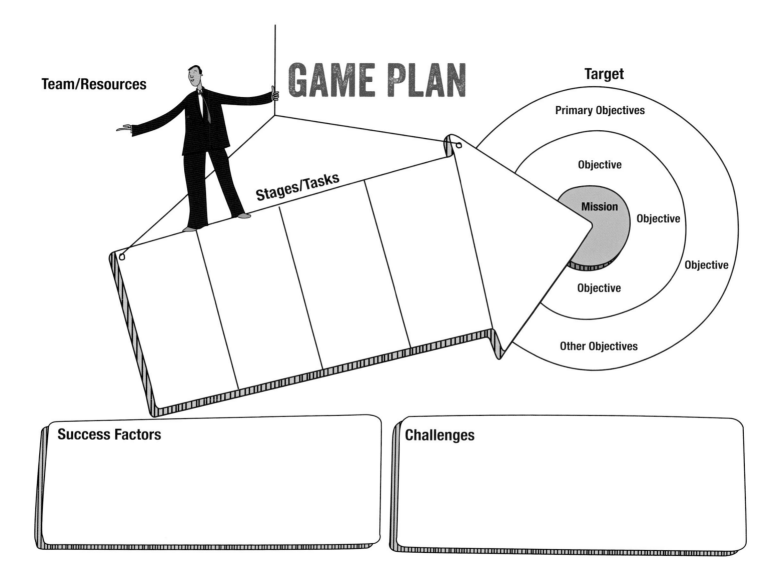

Team/Resources

GAME PLAN

Target

Primary Objectives

Objective

Mission

Objective

Objective

Stages/Tasks

Objective

Objective

Other Objectives

Success Factors

Challenges

Adapted from Game Plan, Grove Consulting visit grove.com for more information - great tools.

GAME PLAN

What is it?

Dave Sibbert and his team have created many fantastic templates you can use to great effect for collaborative planning. Go check them out. I have used them many times to great effect.

Where can I use it?

- For projects of all types, continuous improvement work and team activities – anything that requires a plan.
- As a method for building team alignment around common objectives.
- A fun and effective way to ensure clarity, understanding and meaning
- As a way of strengthening group planning skills.

How do I use it?

- Allow two to three hours for this activity.
- You will need a large sheet of paper with the plan outline drawn on it – preferably A1 or larger and a quantity of marker pens.
- Start with the target area of the plan; clarify the project goal and the specific outcomes and deliverables for the project or activity.
- Then look at the project team, or resources and assess what you have in terms of people, their skills, resources etc.
- For the tasks/project plan area of the plan you will need to ensure the right sequence. Try to keep it top level.
- For the success factors, think about what good will look like when you achieve the goal as well as the shared behaviours and principles that you believe will assist you in being successful.
- Finally identify challenges and kill any risks.

VISIONIT

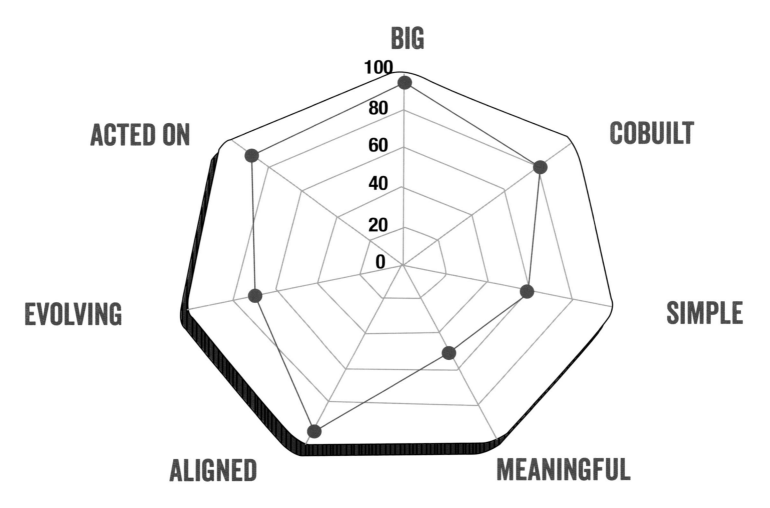

VISIONIT

BIG A powerful vision is bold and exciting. It should make the hairs on the back of your neck stand up. You need to think big!

COBUILT A good vision should be built by the people who are going to live it. Inclusion = Commitment

SIMPLE A powerful vision must be easy to understand and be able to be remembered on a day to day basis.

MEANINGFUL A good vision is understood by everyone in the organisation who can articulate it with meaning and show how they contribute.

ALIGNED A good vision is useless unless there are aligned strategies and plans in place to achieve it. Everything must be focussed in the same direction and momentum created in achieving the vision.

EVOLVING A good vision must evolve as opportunities arrive and conditions change.

ACTED ON For a vision to realise results, people throughout the organisation must act on it and use it as a guiding framework for descion making.

"TALENT WINS GAMES, BUT TEAMWORK AND INTELLIGENCE WINS CHAMPIONSHIPS."

MICHAEL JORDAN

LEADERSHIP TRUTH 3 - BUILD ELITE TEAMS

TEAMWORK

TEAM VITALITY

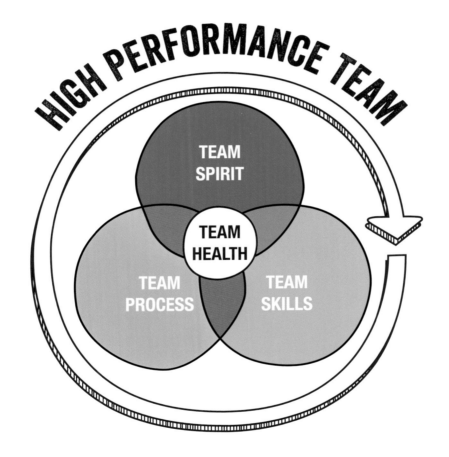

TEAM VITALITY

For a team to be successful it needs to be fantastic in 4 core areas:

1. Team Spirit - clarity of purpose, buy in and proud to be part of the team making a real difference
2. Team Processes - effective and aligned ways of working
3. Team Skills - the right people with the right skills playing to position
4. Team Health - the energy and endurance to sustain high performance

This is the process I use to develop sustainable high performance teams based on the 4 areas.

Unlearning and Learning	Exploring	Visioning	Aligning	Sustaining
Understanding team dynamics in today's world	Team diagnostics	Creating a clear focus	Making the changes required for success	Ensuring the practices and measurements are in place for long term success

Team Kick Start

Themes:

- Importance of teams
- Importance of agility
- Importance of health
- Team types
- High performance model

Team journey introduction

Team Map Produced

The team undertakes a variety of team diagnostics consisting of:

- Individual and team health
- Team alignment
- Team skills
- Team processes
- Team spirit
- Behavioural styles

Individual and team feedback given

Team Visioning

Using a collaborative and interactive process the team develops a clear vision of the future.
It contains:

- Team purpose and Goals
- Guiding Principles
- Key Stakeholders
- Team Ways of Working
- Team RACI
- Value Proposition
- Performance Measures
- Famous for Statement

Team Game Plan

Plan developed to enhance performance based on diagnostics and team vision.

Key areas include

- Team health plan
- Team spirit plan
- Team process plan
- Team skills plan

Team Learning

Key processes and skills developed around reflective practice and action learning.
On-going diagnostics in:

- Health
- Process
- Skills
- Spirit

And of course results...

TEAM PLAYBOOK

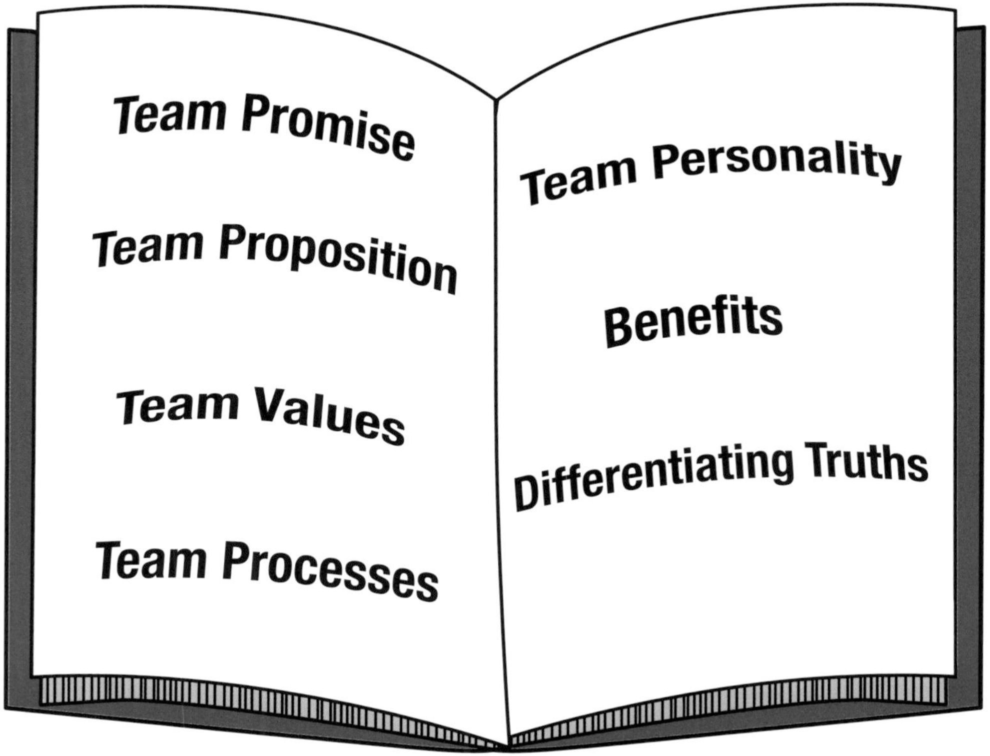

Team Promise

Team Proposition

Team Values

Team Processes

Team Personality

Benefits

Differentiating Truths

TEAM PLAYBOOK

What is it?

It helps to ensure that all involved are clear on where they're heading, how they're going to get there and how they will know when they've arrived! It keeps the team focussed and provides a reference point to remind everyone what was agreed, keeping priorities in everyone's mind. It means that more effective decisions are made, where all individuals are committed to achieving the best result to achieving the teams purpose.

Where can I use it?

- To get off on the right foot when a new team is formed.
- When a team is in trouble and people need to regain their view of the big picture.
- To provide focus, enabling better prioritisation and decision making.
- As a way of capturing what a team is doing really well, so they can continue using their magic formula.
- It can be used for people who work together day to day in teams.
- It can also be used for teams who come together for a specific purpose, such as project teams.
- For teams that work at a distance from one another geographically.
- To provide clarity as changes occur within the organisation, which will impact upon the team.

How do I use it?

- Use the template, ensure everyone involved has view of this template (can be done remotely if needed).
- Ask each question in turn.
- To enable everyone to contribute, ask them to write down their thoughts on Post-It notes as individuals first and stick onto flip chart paper or a wall etc., somewhere visible for everyone.
- Identify any common threads and group these post-its.
- Note in the relevant box on the template. At this stage you may need a page per box in the template.
- Once all questions have been answered bring together the team's thoughts into one place, for example, typing up a page which shows the team's commitments for each of the areas.
- A credit card sized version could be produced for everyone to keep at hand. Send out to everyone involved.
- Refer to this regularly at meetings etc., to keep it fresh and alive. It can be updated if necessary to keep it relevant.

TEAM FLOWS – CREATING A POSITIVE TEAM CLIMATE

Enabling Element	My Actions….
Focus Ensuring your teams have a clear understanding of business goals and direction, why they are important, and how they contribute to achievement	
Learning Ensuring teams and individuals take opportunities to grow and develop through training and self-development, and take responsibility for sharing work based learning with others	
Opportunity Ensuring that teams are able to utilise the full expertise and capability of every team member, and have the autonomy to do so	
Worth Ensuring teams are widely recognised for their capability and achievement, praised and thanked for their efforts and results, and appropriately rewarded for their contribution	
Support Ensuring that every team feels it has the resources, information and management support and commitment it needs to be able to perform at the highest level	

Wyn Llewellyn, Wynmill Consulting

TEAM FLOWS – CREATING A POSITIVE TEAM CLIMATE

What is it?

A framework developed by Wyn Llewellyn for creating a positive team climate. I have used it many times and it works really well.

Where can I use it?

- Team workshops.
- Ongoing review sessions.
- Setting up project environments.

How do I use it?

- Invite team to workshop.
- Set up effective environment to generate ideas.
- Think about what actions you can do for each element and create plan.
- Use the framework on a regular basis to review performance.

Enabling Element	My Actions….
Focus Ensuring your teams have a clear understanding of business goals and direction, why they are important, and how they contribute to achievement	
Learning Ensuring teams and individuals take opportunities to grow and develop through training and self-development, and take responsibility for sharing work based learning with others	
Opportunity Ensuring that teams are able to utilise the full expertise and capability of every team member, and have the autonomy to do so	
Worth Ensuring teams are widely recognised for their capability and achievement, praised and thanked for their efforts and results, and appropriately rewarded for their contribution	
Support Ensuring that every team feels it has the resources, information and management support and commitment it needs to be able to perform at the highest level	

"CREATIVITY IS THINKING UP NEW THINGS. INNOVATION IS DOING NEW THINGS."

THEODORE LEVITT

LEADERSHIP TRUTH 4 - UNLEASH INNOVATION

DISNEY TECHNIQUE

Based on the ideas of Walt Disney

DISNEY TECHNIQUE

What is it?

Disney's thinking technique synthesized three different strategies: the dreamer, realist, and the critic. A dreamer without a realist is often not able to translate fantasies into tangible reality. A dreamer and critic become engaged in constant conflict. A dreamer and realist can create things but find that a critic helps to evaluate and refine the final products.

Why is it important?

• Generating Ideas
• Action Planning

How do I use it?

1. Identify and invite team to workshop. Create three separate areas – one dreaming, one realist and one critic.

2. **DREAMER.** A dreamer spins innumerable fantasies, wishes, outrageous hunches and bold and absurd ideas without limit or judgment. Nothing is censored. Nothing is too absurd or silly. All things are possible for the dreamer. To be the dreamer, ask: If I could wave a magic wand and do anything I want, what would I create? How would it look? What could I do with it? How would it make you feel? What is the most absurd idea I can conceive?

3. **REALIST.** The realist imagineers the dreamer's ideas into something realistic and feasible. He would try to figure out how to make the ideas work and then sort them out in some meaningful order. To be the realist, ask: How can I make this happen? What are the features and aspects of the idea? Can I build ideas from the features or aspects? What is the essence of the idea? Can I extract the principle of the idea? Can I make analogical-metaphorical connections with the principle and something dissimilar to create something tangible? How can I use the essence of the idea to imagineer a more realistic one?

4. **CRITIC.** The critic reviews all the ideas and tries to punch holes in them by playing the devil's advocate. To be the critic, ask: How do I really feel about it? Is this the best I can do? How can I make it better? Does this make sense? How does it look to a customer? A client? An expert? A user? Is it worth my time?

RADIANT PROBLEM SOLVING

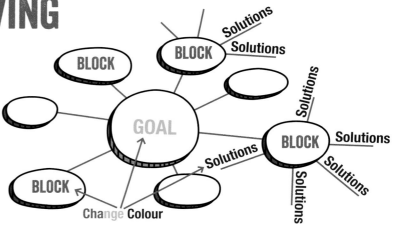

Roles:

Timekeeper - Keep the group to time for each element.
Scribes - Take responsibility for recording ideas
Focus - Ensure that the group is focussed on the right thing. When working on blocks don't discuss solutions and vice versa. Also during the brainstorming sections keep the group to the rules.
Rules of Brainstorming - No analysis, no discussion, no judgement, no right or wrong - record all ideas however wacky!
Reporter - Feedback to other groups, workshop etc.

Process:

Decide on your goal, make sure it is phased as a goal not an issue. Group discussion 5 min.

Brainstorm all the blocks/barriers to achieving your goal. 2 mins.

Take the blocks one at a time and brainstorm all the solutions.
1 min per block.

Review and reflect on the results. Are there common solutions? Can you propose five strategies or next steps to work towards the goal?
5-15 mins.

RADIANT PROBLEM SOLVING

What is it?

Radiant problem solving is a visual collaborative tool to quickly gain ideas of the blockers to achieving a goal and then developing strategies to remove the barriers.

Why is it important?

- Problem Solving
- Action Planning
- Removing barriers to goal achievement

How do I use it?

1. Create right environment with flip chart pens and a team.
2. Decide on goal and write it in the middle of the flip chart/whiteboard.
3. Brainstorm what the team thinks the blockers are to achieving the goal and draw each one of the goal statements in a radial way.
4. With a different coloured pen take each barrier in turn and generate solutions to removing the barrier.
5. Review and agree next steps.

WORLD CAFÉ

Focus on what matters

Notice patterns. Connect ideas

Play.. Draw.. Doodle

doodle

Have fun!

Slow down so you have time to think and reflect

SLOW DOWN

Listen to learn

Contribute your thinking

Speak with your heart and mind

Facilitate yourself with others

WORLD CAFÉ

What is it?

The World Café methodology is a simple, effective, and flexible format for hosting large group dialogue.

Where can I use it?

- Any meeting that requires group debate and collective decision making.
- Can be used as just one part of a larger meeting.

How do I use it?

World Café can be modified to meet a wide variety of needs. Specifics of context, numbers, purpose, location, and other circumstances are factored into each event's unique invitation, design, and question choice, but the following five components comprise the basic model:

Setting: Create a "special" environment, most often modelled after a café, i.e. small round tables covered with a paper tablecloth, coloured pens, a vase of flowers, and optional "talking stick" item. There should be four chairs at each table.

Welcome and Introduction: The host begins with a warm welcome and an introduction to the World Café process, setting the context, sharing the Cafe Etiquette, and putting participants at ease.

Small Group Rounds: The process begins with the first of three or more rounds (length of time chosen by facilitator) of conversation for the small group seated around a table. At the end of the round, each member of the group moves to the next table. They may or may not choose to leave one person as the "table host" for the next round, who welcomes the next group and briefly fills them in on what happened in the previous round.

Questions: Each round is prefaced with a question designed for the specific context and desired purpose of the session. The same questions can be used for more than one round, or they can be built upon each other to focus the conversation or guide its direction.

Harvest: After the small groups (and/or in between rounds, as desired) individuals are invited to share insights or other results from their conversations with the rest of the large group. These results are reflected visually in a variety of ways.

theworldcafe.com is well worth a visit to explore this great process, I use it all the time.

"TAKE ADVANTAGE OF THE AMBIGUITY IN THE WORLD. LOOK AT SOMETHING AND THINK WHAT ELSE IT MIGHT BE."

ROGER VON OECH

LEADERSHIP TRUTH 5 - MANAGE AMBIGUITY AND KILL RISK

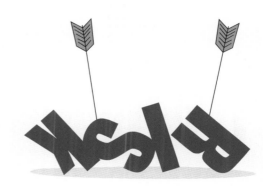

DILEMMAS

Key question: How do we create a solution based on the best of both?

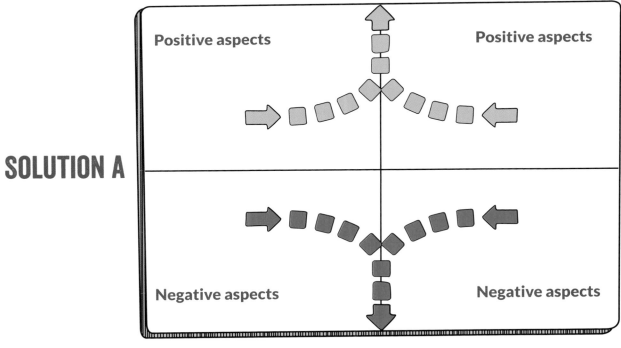

DILEMMAS

What is it?

Dilemmas is a way to structure conversation to ensure people get clarity and understanding of the tensions in the business. It helps to promote AND thinking and understanding of the challenges.

An example dilemma could be the question, "Do we centralise or de-centralise?" Dilemmas helps you create solutions that achieve the best of both. For example the question should be, "How do we create an organisation that has the best of control and the best of empowerment?" Mapping out the dilemma using the template helps with discussion and understanding.

I have found it useful to convert what is complex and hard to define into something that is simple to see while raising awareness to a deeper level.

Where can I use it?

• Conflict resolution
• Create solutions
• Help explore strategies
• Give meaning
• Remove ambiguity and confusion

How do I use it?

1 Identify key stakeholders and invite to workshop
2. Explain concept
3. Using post it notes to brainstorm tensions
4. Review and create action plan to manage tensions

ORGANISATIONAL ALIGNMENT

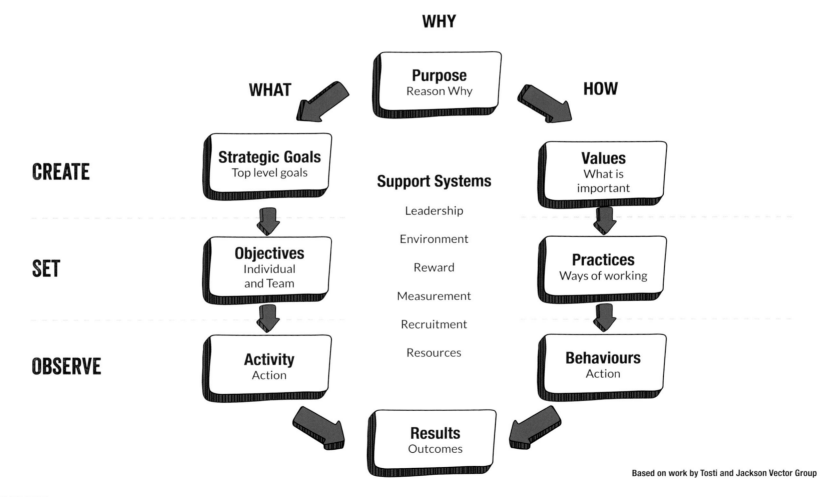

WHY

WHAT

HOW

Purpose
Reason Why

CREATE

Strategic Goals
Top level goals

Support Systems

Leadership

Values
What is
important

Environment

SET

Objectives
Individual
and Team

Reward

Measurement

Practices
Ways of working

OBSERVE

Activity
Action

Recruitment

Resources

Behaviours
Action

Results
Outcomes

Based on work by Tosti and Jackson Vector Group

ORGANISATIONAL ALIGNMENT

What is it?

A framework that helps to ensure efficiency is achieved through alignment. It can be used at organisational level all the way through to an individual level.

Where can I use it?

1. Planning and implementing strategy
2. Setting up teams
3. Reducing waste
4. Changing behaviour
5. Improving performance
6. Coaching

How do I use it?

1. Create clarity around your purpose, values and goals.
2. Set with your team objectives and ways of working that align to your purpose, values and goals.
3. Ensure your support systems are aligned.
4. Observe your team to ensure the right activities are done and the right behaviours demonstrated.
5. If not then analyse the system first and see what needs aligning before blaming people.

ANTICIPATING AND KILLING RISK

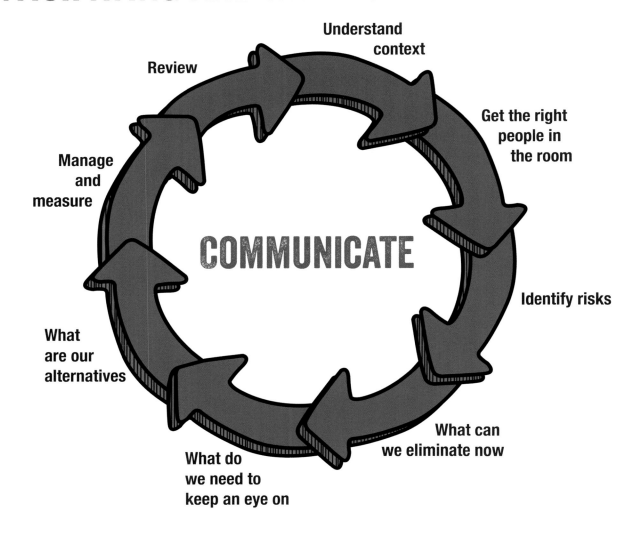

ANTICIPATING & KILLING RISK

What is it?

A process that guides you to ensuring risks are managed effectively.

Where can I use it?

- The process can be used during any situation requiring you to plan outcomes and manage risks:
- Strategic Planning
- Programme Management
- Project Management
- Leading Teams

How do I use it?

1. Take time to fully understand the context you are in and how what you are doing links to the strategy
2. Identify who should be involved in analysing the risks - usually the people closest to the problem.
3. Run workshop to identify risks and generate actions to eliminate as many as you can. Build ideas into plans.
4. For the risks that can't be resolved you need to agree how you are going to minimise the impact and keep an eye on them.
5. If the risks happen what are your alternatives, what else can you do to reach your objectives.
6. Now manage and measure risks on an ongoing basis.
7. Conduct regular reviews with the people who matter.
8. Take ongoing action to remove risks.

"THE JOB OF AN EDUCATOR IS TO TEACH STUDENTS TO SEE VITALITY IN THEMSELVES."

JOSEPH CAMPBELL

LEADERSHIP TRUTH 6 - EDUCATE

LEADER MANAGER COACH

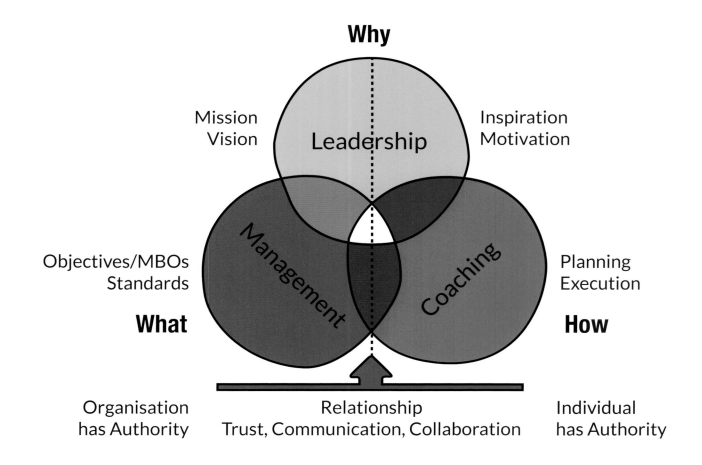

Why

Mission
Vision

Leadership

Inspiration
Motivation

Objectives/MBOs
Standards

Management

Coaching

Planning
Execution

What

How

Organisation
has Authority

Relationship
Trust, Communication, Collaboration

Individual
has Authority

LEADER MANAGER COACH

What is it?

A model which illustrates the role of a 'Leader of People', which helps you understand how Leadership, Management and Coaching, built on a foundation of strong relationships, work together to help create the conditions for sustained high performance.

3 Roles:

1: Leader. Why? The Purpose. A leader needs to work towards a purpose and vision, and inspire and motivate people on that journey.

2: Manager. What? The Goals to be achieved. The vision needs to be cascaded to a business or team structure, goals and objectives e.g. MBOs.

3: Coach. How? The Planning and Execution. Individuals need to plan and implement in a way that makes full use of their own experience, skills and creativity, which a 'leader of people' can support through coaching.

Relationships: The three roles work together but require different approaches and skills. To be effective in these three roles it is essential that your relationships are built on strong foundations e.g. trust, collaboration and communication. When the three are in harmony, you create the conditions for high performance in others.

Authority: Effective organisations that sustain long-term performance have a balanced relationship between the organisation and the individual. Organisations have the authority to set a vision, goals and create standards and rules. Individuals have authority over (are the 'author' of) their own motivation and use of their experience, skills and creativity. The line down the middle of the diagram illustrates this balance. For example as a Manager you predominantly have organisational authority to set goals in line with the company's vision (WHAT needs to be achieved); as a Coach you must empower individuals to use their own resources as much as possible to enable them to have more authority over HOW they achieve the goals.

Where Can I Use it?

Reviewing my role/s as a leader of people, where I focus my attention and energy, where I should be, and where there are gaps I need to fill.

How do I use it?

- How do I see my role as a 'leader of people?' Do I tend to see my role as more of a manager? A coach? A leader? A relationship builder?
- Where do I tend to put my focus and energy? Think about the conversations you have with your team, are these conversations based more on leadership, management or coaching? What would your team say?
- To keep balance, considering both your role and your strengths, where would you like to put more focus and energy?
- How can you do this?

LEADER MANAGER COACH

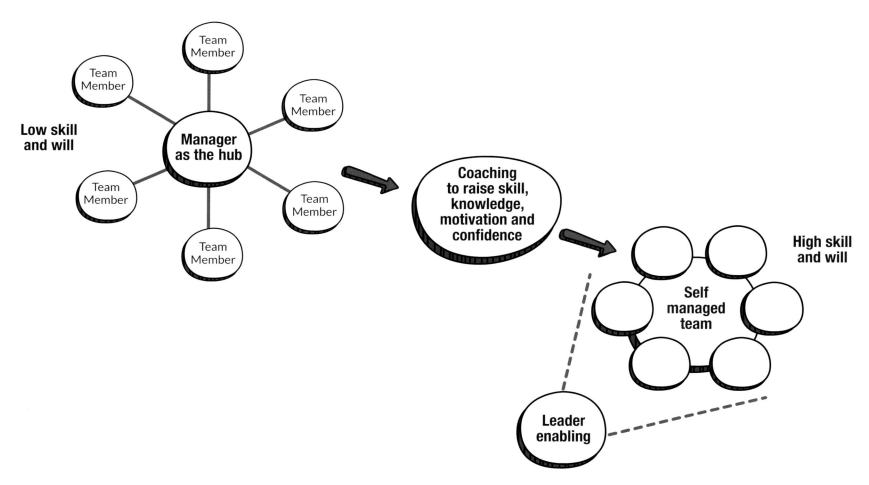

LEADER MANAGER COACH EXAMPLES

Leader

Creating vision and strategy

Communicating and setting direction

Motivating action

Aligning people

Creating systems that managers can manage and transforming them when needed to allow for growth, evolution, opportunities, and hazard avoidance

Inspires trust

Drives innovation

Manages today and builds tomorrow

Longer term perspective

Manager

Planning and budgeting

Organising and staffing

Controlling and problem solving

Leads through position

Taking complex systems of people and technology and making them run efficiently and effectively, hour after hour, day after day

Maintains status quo

Get things done

Manages and improves today

Short term perspective

Coach

Raises awareness for the need to develop by asking questions

Builds responsibility to change by asking questions

Asks questions to challenge and provoke action

Only offers help if asked for or is needed

Develops capability

Improves confidence

Increases capability

Improves skills and ability

Has conversations that improve performance

PAC FACTOR – INCREASING PERSONAL MOTIVATION

Area	
PURPOSE	Increase purpose by …
ATTITUDE	Maintain a positive attitude by…
CONFIDENCE	Improve confidence by…

PAC FACTOR – INCREASING PERSONAL MOTIVATION

What is it?

• A tool for increasing personal motivation.

Where can I use it?

• Personal Development.
• 121 Coaching.
• Team Development.

How do I use it?

Review each element and develop actions.
Example actions:

Increasing purpose
• Goal setting
• Understanding purpose
• Link action to strategy
• Process mapping
• Role definition

Developing positive attitude
• Training
• Coaching
• Build awareness
• Talk to positive people
• Read inspiring stories

Increasing confidence
• High challenge and high support
• Set stretch goals
• Review successes and understand why successful
• Create an action plan and carry out regular reviews

ACTION LEARNING

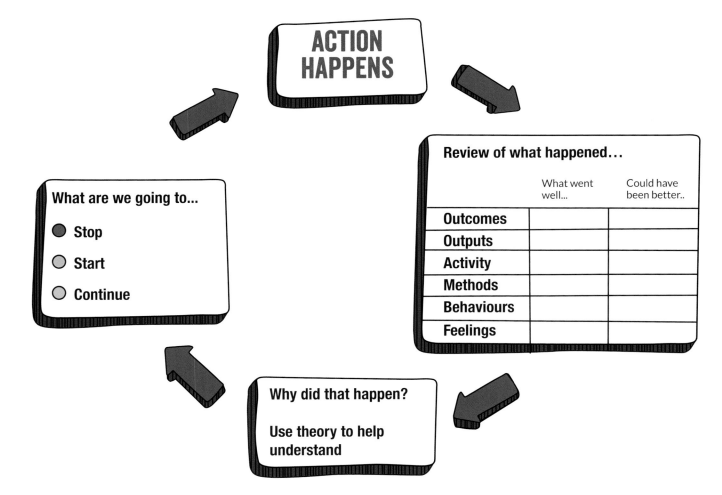

ACTION HAPPENS

Review of what happened...

	What went well...	Could have been better..
Outcomes		
Outputs		
Activity		
Methods		
Behaviours		
Feelings		

Why did that happen?

Use theory to help understand

What are we going to...
- Stop
- Start
- Continue

ACTION LEARNING

What is it?

• A tool for reviewing and learning from any action to ensure continuous improvement happens..

Where can I use it?

• To review any type of action or activity.
• To challenge any existing ways of working.
• Either as an individual or as a team.
• As a pragmatic way of encouraging a more effective approach.
• At the end of a meeting.
• Project reviews.

How do I use it?

• Prepare sheets of paper and some pens – where this is being completed in a team, or group situation it is best to use flip chart paper/paper show/whiteboard.
• Start by talking through the action, or activity that has taken place and be clear on what happened.
• Understand and agree what went well and not so well under the headings of outcomes, outputs, methods, behaviours and feelings.
• Now take each one in turn and consider why in this case – what made the success a success? What caused the elements that did not go so well to be a challenge? It is important to get to the root cause of both the successes and challenges as this will enable real learning to be taken.
• Once all the areas have been discussed you can consider and reach agreement on what, as a result should be stopped, started and continued.

LEARNING CYCLE

Learning x Connection x Action = Impact
More 'Cycles' = More Impact

Learn

- Expose Yourself To Learning Situations
- Actively Process: Observe, Listen, Reflect
- Make It Social: Share, Contribute, Question
- Make It Creative: Generate Ideas
- Make It Real : Translate To Your World

LEARNING IMPACT

Connect

- Meaning: What Meaning Does This Have For Me Personally?
- Impact: What Impact Could This Have on Achieving My Goals?
- Relationships: How Does This Relate to Other Things I Think, Feel, or Do?
- Interest: What's Most Interesting?

Act

- Plan: What, When, Who With, How?
- Take 'Safe' Steps
- Blocks: What or Who May Block?
- Facilitators: What or Who Will Help?
- Deliberate Practice
- Be Bold

LEARNING CYCLE

What is it?

- It is a model to help you understand the importance of 'complete learning' and how you can take ownership for increasing the impact of your learning.
- Learning how to learn or 'meta-learning' has been shown to significantly increase learning and its impact.
- Learning in itself can be a purely academic exercise. In a business context it is not the end goal. Learning must have an impact, which usually involves a change in behaviour, leading to increased performance and progression.
- Behaviour changes when people 'connect' with learning in meaningful ways, they challenge themselves and they take action to do new and different things.

Where can I use it?

- When thinking about how to maximise the impact of learning, to increase performance and progression, either for yourself or others.

How do I use it?

1 Familiarise yourself with the steps in the cycle, all of which have been shown to increase the impact of learning.
2 Use this model in conjunction with your Personal Development Plan (PDP) and Learning Logs, in the Further Resources section:
   - Use your PDP to plan how you can expose yourself to the most relevant sources of learning.
   - Use your learning log to review, form connections with, and plan implementation of learning.
3 Remember that development comes from repeated experience.

BUILDING CONFIDENCE: MIND-SET ZONES

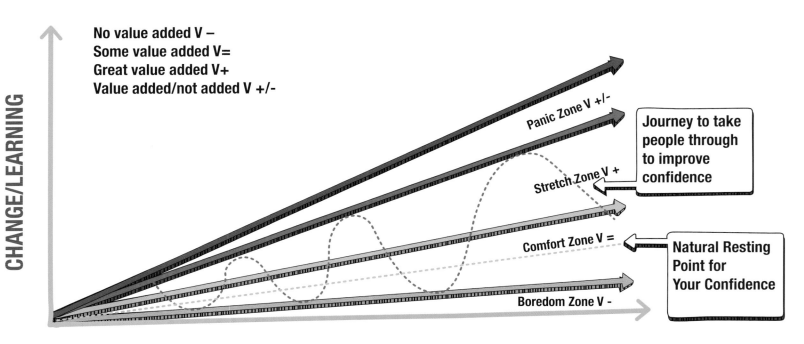

No value added V −
Some value added V=
Great value added V+
Value added/not added V +/-

CHANGE/LEARNING

Panic Zone V +/-

Journey to take people through to improve confidence

Stretch Zone V +

Comfort Zone V =

Natural Resting Point for Your Confidence

Boredom Zone V -

TIME

BUILDING CONFIDENCE: MIND-SET ZONES

What is it?

• A way to visualise how to improve the confidence of individuals and teams.

Where can I use it?

• Personal development.
• 121 coaching.
• Team development

How do I use it?

• The key to building confidence in people is to create a high challenge and high support environment to enable people to come out of their comfort zone.
• Break the journey down into small chunks of challenge. Don't do it all in one go.
• Once a chunk is completed conduct an after action review to draw out the learning and the realisation of what has been achieved. Celebrate success and learning.
• If not successful set another challenge at the same level and support.
• When successful set the next challenge which should be a little harder then repeat process.

"GOOD BUSINESS LEADERS CREATE A VISION, ARTICULATE THE VISION, PASSIONATELY OWN THE VISION, AND RELENTLESSLY DRIVE IT TO COMPLETION."

JACK WELSH

LEADERSHIP TRUTH 7 - EXECUTE WITH PACE

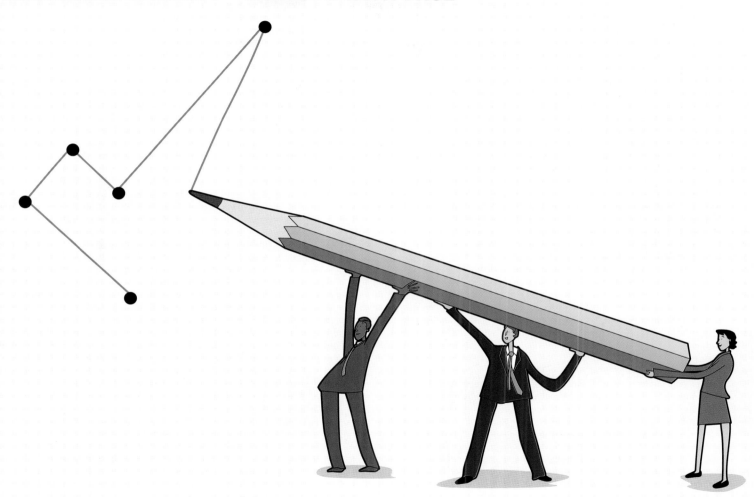

PROJECT FRAMEWORK

**Project working and thinking is becoming more and more important for leaders in today's world.
Here is a simple framework to help guide you through delivering outstanding outcomes.**

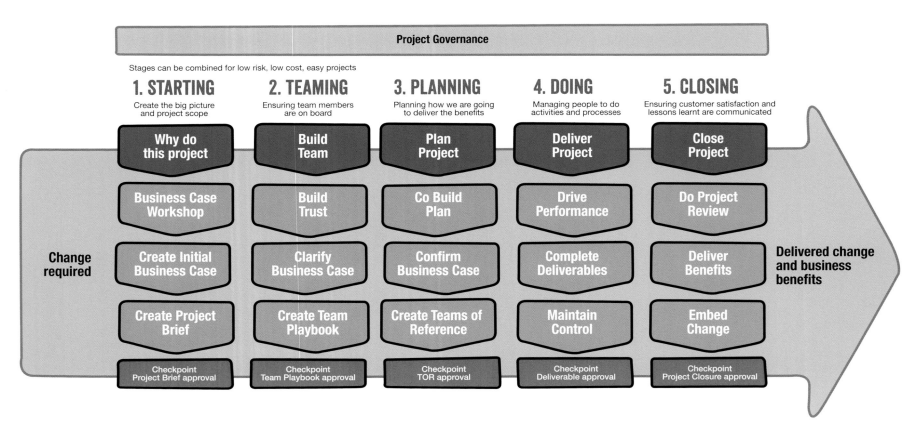

Project Governance

Stages can be combined for low risk, low cost, easy projects

1. STARTING	2. TEAMING	3. PLANNING	4. DOING	5. CLOSING
Create the big picture and project scope	Ensuring team members are on board	Planning how we are going to deliver the benefits	Managing people to do activities and processes	Ensuring customer satisfaction and lessons learnt are communicated
Why do this project	Build Team	Plan Project	Deliver Project	Close Project
Business Case Workshop	Build Trust	Co Build Plan	Drive Performance	Do Project Review
Create Initial Business Case	Clarify Business Case	Confirm Business Case	Complete Deliverables	Deliver Benefits
Create Project Brief	Create Team Playbook	Create Teams of Reference	Maintain Control	Embed Change
Checkpoint Project Brief approval	Checkpoint Team Playbook approval	Checkpoint TOR approval	Checkpoint Deliverable approval	Checkpoint Project Closure approval

Change required

Delivered change and business benefits

PROJECT FRAMEWORK

What is it?

• A simple and very effective project management guide

Where can I use it?

• Setting up and running projects.

How do I use it?

• The framework is part of a project toolkit I have developed. Each stage has a guide and set of documents and tools to help you.
• Here are a few key elements to keep in mind:
  - First of all the project is owned by a sponsor - find out who that is and make them aware of their role.
  - Understand what the governance controls are.
  - Before rushing into deliver make sure you go through each of the first three stages, scoping, teaming and planning.
  - Never start delivering until you have an agreed terms of reference.
  - Make sure the customer is involved early on.
  - Start with winning the business over early on so they understand why you are doing it.
  - Education first then build the solution - the customer should be begging you for a solution.
  - Break the project into stages.
  - Co-building the plan with stakeholders is vital.
  - Deliver through your team to ensure you have time to think.
  - Kill any risk early on.
  - Make sure you know who is responsible for benefits delivery.
  - Review and learn regularly.
  - Evolve plans as you go along.
  - Decide on the methodology based on the situation you are in.
  - Have fun and learn lots.

LIFE OF A MEETING

What does a great meeting look like?

The most important thing to remember is that success is defined by what happens after the meeting! When I am teaching leaders how to plan, prepare and conduct a meeting that inspires action I start with drawing what a meeting should look like and what happens in reality.

Question
How do you run your meetings, green or purple line?

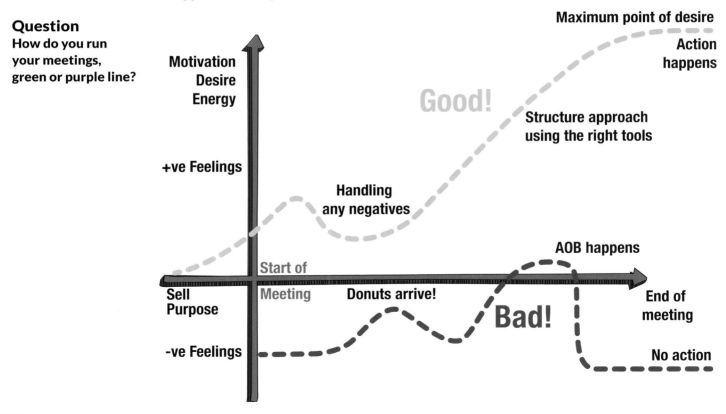

MEETING PROCESS

PLAN **START** **CONDUCT** **CLOSE** **FOLLOW-UP**

PLAN	START	CONDUCT	CLOSE	FOLLOW-UP
• Clarify meeting purpose and outcomes	• Check in	• Cover one item at a time	• Summarise decisions	• Distribute notes and actions promptly
• Identify meeting participants	• Review agenda	• Manage discussions	• Review action items	• File agendas, notes and other documents
• Select methods to meet purpose	• Set or review ground rules	• Maintain focus and pace	• Solicit agenda items for next meeting	• Do assignments
• Develop and distribute agendas	• Clarify roles	• Maintain energy	• Review time and place for next meeting	• Review, Learn, Apply
• Set up room	• Handle any negatives early	• On-going review	• Evaluate the meeting	• Hold each other accountable
		• Facilitate process	• Thank participants	
			• Urge for action	

"THE BAD NEWS IS THAT TIME FLIES, THE GOOD NEWS IS THAT YOU ARE THE PILOT" ANON.

MEETING PREPARATION

The success of a meeting is largely determined by the preparation done in advance.
These questions are designed to help you think through the key considerations.

Question	Guide
Do I really need the meeting?	What do I want to happen as a result? How does this link to my strategy/plans/organisational strategy? Can I achieve this without the cost of a face to face meeting?
What do I want to achieve?	What are the specific goals of the meeting? What type of meeting is it?
Who do I need at the meeting?	Who are the key stakeholders, decision makers, experts, influencers? Any politics I need to handle?
When is the best time?	Avoid clashes with other meetings, when do I need the decisions by? What time of day is best? Anything else going on that will impact on results?
Where is the best place to run it?	On site, off site, which country, transport links, environment, customer base?
What is the best process?	Flow of pre, during and post process. Which tools will work best? What order? How do I create buy in and a sense of urgency?
Do I know expectations of participants?	What are the hopes and fears of participants? What issues do they have? What opportunities are they looking for?
What conversations are needed?	Is it information sharing? Is it a brainstorm/creative session? Or to test an idea? Consultation? Inclusive planning meeting? Create something together? Review and learn meeting?
How will decisions get made?	Executive, rule based, consensus
What documentation format?	Who will use it? How will it be used? When needed?
What follow up is required?	What is the best communication method? Intranet, email, telecom, face to face?

MEETING AGENDA TEMPLATE

Meeting Name:

Purpose:
Date:
Location:
Start and Finish Times:
Who is attending:
Meeting Roles:

Timing	Topic (written as a question)	Who Leads	How (tools, technique, process)	Expected Outcomes

STORYBOARDING

Outcomes.

STORYBOARDING

What is it?

- A simple and very effective planning tool.
- A fun and effective method for starting with the end in mind and working backwards to the detailed activity required to achieve this outcome.

Where can I use it?

- For planning almost any type of desired outcome.
- Used prior to meeting to plan activities and flow.
- Used to plan an action plan at end of a meeting.
- Particularly good for crafting solutions to sticky situations.
- Either individually or with a team.

How do I use it?

- Using the template as a guide prepare a number of large sheets of paper - at least A3 and gather a selection of Post-it notes.
- Start with the end in mind and describe what needs to have been delivered in terms of outcomes.
- Using Post-it notes brainstorm the activities that need to have happened in order for the outcome/s to be achieved.
- Then create your storyboard sequence by moving the post notes around to create the right flow. It is a good idea to do this a few times with a break between to fully synthesise the information. Then draw up a neat version of the storyboard with a time line and actions.

DIRECT GOAL SETTING

DREAM BASED
INSPIRING BASED
ROUTE BASED
EMOTION BASED
CHALLENGE BASED
THINKING BASED

DIRECT GOAL SETTING

What is it?

• A framework that helps you set inspiring goals and a plan.

Where can I use it?

1. Any situation requiring you to develop goals
2. Coaching

How do I use it?

Create space and time to think. Make sure you feel energised and relaxed.

Use the headings as a guide to help formulate your goals and plan.

Dream based - all goals should be purpose led and based on big stuff that really matters to you.

Inspiring based - they should make the hairs on the back of your neck stand up!

Route based - there should be a method crafted to achieve your dream.

Emotion based - they should indicate what emotions you need to create to achieve your dreams - what person do you need to be in order to achieve what you want.

Challenge based - they should be stretching and out there way beyond your comfort zone. Fear after all is fun in disguise; and it is where the magic happens!

Thinking based - they should outline the type of thinking you need to drive the right actions.

DRIVERS FOR CHANGE DR x IV x ERS x CAP = REAL CHANGE

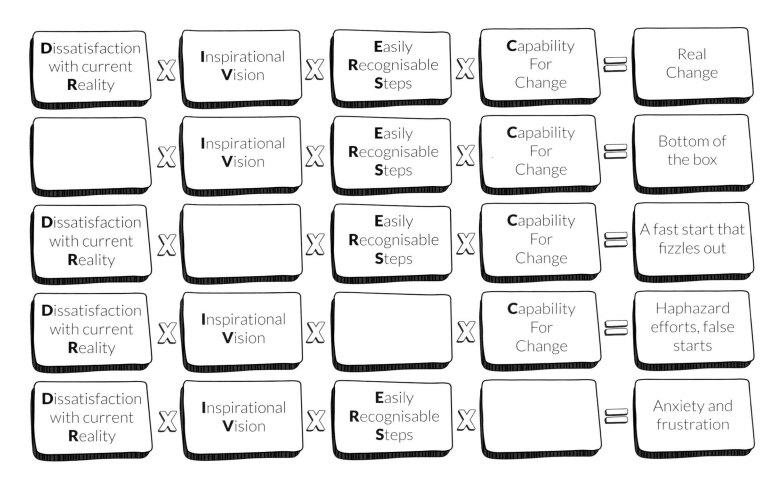

Dissatisfaction with current **R**eality	X **I**nspirational **V**ision	X **E**asily **R**ecognisable **S**teps	X **C**apability For Change	= Real Change
	X **I**nspirational **V**ision	X **E**asily **R**ecognisable **S**teps	X **C**apability For Change	= Bottom of the box
Dissatisfaction with current **R**eality	X	X **E**asily **R**ecognisable **S**teps	X **C**apability For Change	= A fast start that fizzles out
Dissatisfaction with current **R**eality	X **I**nspirational **V**ision	X	X **C**apability For Change	= Haphazard efforts, false starts
Dissatisfaction with current **R**eality	X **I**nspirational **V**ision	X **E**asily **R**ecognisable **S**teps	X	= Anxiety and frustration

DRIVERS FOR CHANGE

What is it?

A framework that illustrates the four key elements that need to be in place when making change happen.

Where can I use it?

1. Any situation requiring you to develop a change plan.
2. When you are reviewing a change initiative.

How do I use it?

- Putting together a change plan

1. Make sure you understand the purpose and need for change. How will this change support the strategy?
2. Identify key stakeholders and invite to workshop.
3. Identify actions for each element of the framework.
4. Develop plan to ensure all four elements are met.
5. Communicate and engage people in the plan.

- Reviewing a change initiative

1. Observe behaviours in people being impacted by the change and teams making change happen.
2. Use the behaviours to understand what elements are missing .
3. Challenge change team to demonstrate what they have done to ensure each element is in place.
4. Develop next steps together.

DR x IV x ERS x CAP = REAL CHANGE

COACHING CHANGE

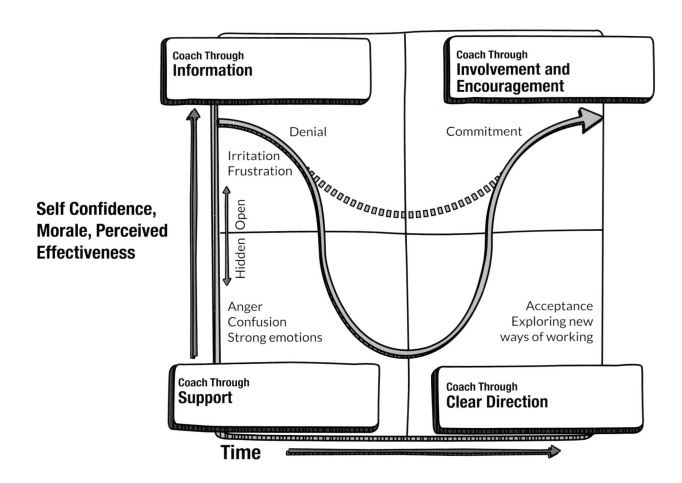

Coach Through
Information

Coach Through
Involvement and Encouragement

Denial

Irritation
Frustration

Commitment

Hidden | Open

Self Confidence, Morale, Perceived Effectiveness

Anger
Confusion
Strong emotions

Acceptance
Exploring new ways of working

Coach Through
Support

Coach Through
Clear Direction

Time

COACHING CHANGE

What is it?

A model of change showing the physical and emotional states that people are likely to go through when dealing with any kind of significant change. It is based on a model originally developed in the 1960s by Elizabeth Kubler-Ross and is now widely used as a method for helping people to understand their reactions to significant change or upheaval.

Where can I use it?

- Each person reacts differently to change and not all will experience every phase of the change curve. People also move through the phases at different speeds. Understanding this can help you to decide how and when to communicate information to individuals.

- It can assist you in considering what level of support someone requires.

- It is a useful tool for individual and team change.

How do I use it?

You will not require any specific resources to use this tool – just an understanding of how you can manage each phase. At the first stage when there is a requirement for information, it is a good idea to give the individual as much information as you can about what the change is, and why it is taking place, what the benefits are for them and the business, when the change is happening and what the impact is for them.

Provide answers to their questions honestly and openly and help then to understand what's in it for them. In the second stage they will need support. It is important to understand what support they require and provide this for them wherever possible. There maybe others within the business or outside that can provide this. As they move through there will become a need to manage them through clear direction. This will be at the point where they start to accept the changes and they will be looking for clarity on new ways of working and the next steps for them as an individual. They will be finding ways to deal with the new reality and knowing what they need to do differently will help them.

The last phase requires involvement and encouragement. Involve them in the change as much as possible to make them feel a part of it. Encourage them to develop new, relevant skills that will benefit them.

CHALLENGE VS SUPPORT

Support — High / Low

COMFORT

PERFORMANCE

APATHY

STRESS

Challenge — Low / High

CHALLENGE VS SUPPORT

What is it?

A framework to remind us that high performance requires high challenge and high support.

Where can I use it?

- Planning action.
- Team development.
- Performance management.
- Coaching.

How do I use it?

1. Stop and review actions about to be taken.
2. Review actions based on model and ensure high challenge and high support has been met.
3. Review and gain feedback.
4. Observe team and adjust as necessary.

CHANGE BRIDGE

CHANGE BRIDGE

What is it?

• A visual tool to identify where people are with the project/
task or role.

Where can I use it?

• At the start of a project, meeting or event.
• During various review stages to assess how people are feeling about
what is happening.

How do I use it?

This can be done as printed images or projected onto a whiteboard.
Ask individuals to add their name/initials/colour in the character which
best shows how they feel in regards to your situation. For example
'when you were told about the changes ahead how did you feel?' Give
them a minute or two to scan the diagram and think about why they are
choosing that particular character.

Then go round the group asking them to identify their character and
explain why it has been chosen. For example with Character A they may
say that 'they can see the end result, feel happy about their involvement
in it and exciting about sharing the results'.

Keep the diagram and at various relevant stages of the project ask them
to complete another and compare how they are now feeling. A People
identifying B & C may need more support.

JOURNEY MAP

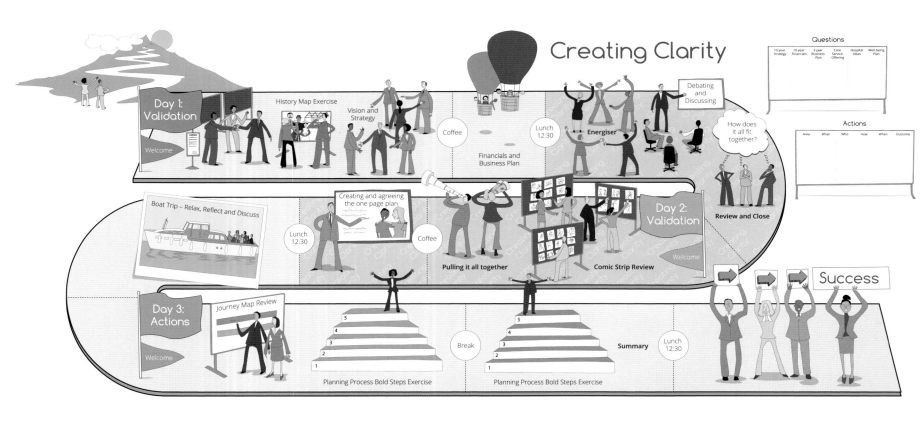

JOURNEY MAP

What is it?

- A visual tool for capturing the key messages and learning from the events that took place or are about to take place.

Where can I use it?

- To review or communicate any type of action or activity.
- Either as an individual or as a team.
- As a pragmatic way of encouraging a more effective approach.
- At the start of a meeting/workshop.
- Project kick offs or reviews.

How do I use it?

- Sheets of paper and some pens – where this is being completed in a team, or group situation it is best to use flip chart paper/ paper show/ whiteboard.
- Start by talking through the action or activity that has taken place and be clear on what happened or is going to happen.
- Using pictures and as few words as possible sketch/draw/doodle/ create a visual time-line of the event being reviewed. This should form a sequence like a comic strip or story board.
- Pictures should be used as metaphors to the facts, findings, feelings and lessons learnt during the event.
- Review the journey map by sharing with individuals, the wider team or any other appropriate audience.

EASE IMPACT GRID

1. My key learning points…

1
2
3
4
5
6

3. My game plan…

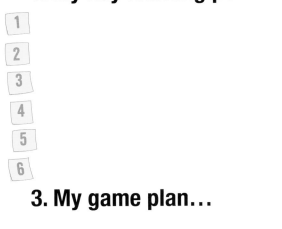

2. My prioritised list…

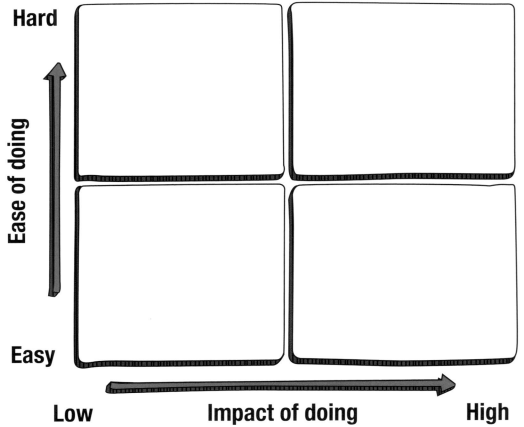

Hard

Easy

Ease of doing

Low

Impact of doing

High

EASE IMPACT GRID

What is it?

• A tool for prioritising actions

Where can I use it?

• To develop an action plan
• Game plan

How do I use it?

• Prepare sheets of paper and some pens – where this is being completed in a team, or group situation it is best to use flip chart paper.
• Start by listing key learning points and then number them.
• Then populate the grid based on how easy it is to do and the impact of doing it.
• Develop actions to implement learning:

1. Quick wins – easy to do with a high impact

2. Longer term plans – hard to do with a high impact

3. Low hanging fruit – easy to do with a low impact

4. Disregard if possible – hard to do with a low impact

LEADERSHIP STYLES

COACHING

Directing
Provide specific instructions and closely supervise

Facilitate improved learning, development and performance through raising awareness, expanding thinking, encouraging and supporting

Delegating
Hand over responsibility for implementation

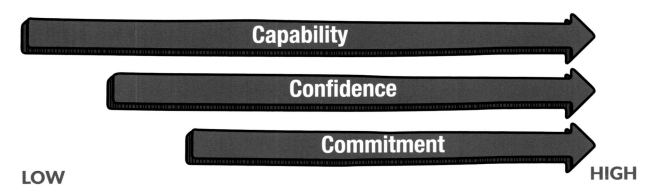

Capability

Confidence

Commitment

LOW

HIGH

LEADERSHIP STYLES

What is it?

• A tool ensuring you use the correct leadership style.

Where can I use it?

In any influencing situation that requires:

• Directing
• Coaching
• Delegating

How do I use it?

It is useful to keep in mind that there is no 'best way' to influence in a leadership situation. Your leadership behaviour may be more or less effective depending on the readiness of the person/team you are leading.

1. Establish the specific task, job, activity you need completing.
2. Assess the readiness the team or individual has for that task (Capability, Commitment, Confidence).
3. Select the right style for the situation (Directing, Coaching, Delegating).
4. The aim is to move people along the spectrum as their capability, confidence and commitment grow, allowing more empowerment and accountability.

Capability - the knowledge, skills and ability the person has to complete the task.
Confidence - the self belief the person has to complete the task.
Commitment - the motivation and drive the person has to complete the task.

1. Capability

The higher someone's capability, the less directive you need to be and the more you can empower the individual to complete their own tasks with less intervention and support.

2. Confidence

If someone's confidence is low, you may need to be more supportive and offer more direction than their capability may otherwise indicate. A Coaching style rather than Directing is likely to be more appropriate as coaching support is more likely to help build confidence.

3. Commitment

If someone's commitment is low, you may also need to be more directive and supportive, but to a lesser degree, as they need to take accountability for their own commitment and performance. Feedback and clarification of expectations, as part of a coaching approach are a good starting point.

FURTHER RESOURCES

Leadership Laid Bare is the first in a series of leadership books designed to start a LEADERSHIP REVOLUTION.

Ebooks available are:

Meetings That ROCK! How to plan, prepare and conduct meetings that inspire action

Elite Teams: How to build an Elite Team and sustain performance

Strategic Innovation Unleashed: How to generate ideas and land them to create value

Performance Conversations: How to effortlessly drive performance through conversations

ChangePro: Complete guide to lead perfect projects that deliver every time

Negotiate: How to achieve 'win more - win more' outcomes

There are more toolkits being developed all the time, so make sure check out grahamwilson.com.

#LEADERSHIPREVOLUTION

WORKING WITH ME

I run a small number of very select mastermind groups per year with a maximum of seven people per group. The key is the quality of people put together to form the perfect group to learn with and from each other. My mastermind groups meet for two days every quarter for full immersion workshops. This requires total commitment to the group. They are not for the faint hearted or people just playing at developing as a leader.

I also run the occasional three day open leadership programme to encourage a wide range of different organisations and cultures to collide and make leadership magic happen.

Added to this I coach a maximum of seven hand picked people per year. This ensures the results are extraordinary!

The rest of my working time is focussed on developing leadership teams of global brands.

IF YOU ARE INTERESTED IN WORKING WITH ME PLEASE GET IN CONTACT @ GRAHAMWILSON.COM

IMAGINE A WORLD WHERE ...

PEOPLE FEEL INSPIRED TO DO GREAT WORK

LEADERS ENABLE SUCCESS

BOLDNESS, SIMPLICITY AND SPEED ARE THE NORM

PURPOSE IS CLEAR

WORK IS PURPOSEFUL, FUN AND ENGAGING

LEADERS FEEL COMFORTABLE BEING THEMSELVES

LEADERS BUILD A HIGH TRUST ENVIRONMENT

LEADERSHIP LAID BARE

THE NAKED TRUTH OF WHAT GREAT LEADERS ACTUALLY DO

"THEY CREATE A HIGH PERFORMANCE ENVIRONMENT WHERE SUCCESS IS INEVITABLE"

1 **LEADERSHIP PURPOSE:**
THEY AWAKEN POSSIBILITY IN PEOPLE TO DELIVER EXTRAORDINARY RESULTS

3 **LEADERSHIP PRINCIPLES:**
THEY OPERATE WITH BOLDNESS, SIMPLICITY AND SPEED

7 **LEADERSHIP TRUTHS:**
THEY LIVE THE 7 TIMELESS LEADERSHIP PRINCIPLES

1 THEY UNDERSTAND THEMSELVES AND HAVE A STORY TO TELL:
THEY HAVE AN AUTHENTIC LEADERSHIP BRAND, THEY BUILD ON STRENGTHS, THEY ARE HAPPY BEING VULNERABLE, THEY ARE THEMSELVES, THEY SHARE THEIR LEADERSHIP PHILOSOPHY, THEY BUILD TRUST, THEY ARE POSITIVE, HEALTHY AND HAPPY.

2 THEY INSPIRE ACTION:
PURPOSE IS AT THE HEART OF EVERYTHING THEY DO, THEY MAKE A DIFFERENCE, THEY HAVE COURAGE, THEY GO OUT ON A LIMB, THEY ARE BOLD, THEY TELL STORIES AND GIVE EXAMPLES THAT GIVE MEANING AND INSPIRE ACTION. THEY CREATE A SENSE OF REAL VALUE.

INNOVATION

TEAMWORK

4 THEY UNLEASH INNOVATION:
THEY CREATE A CULTURE WHERE EVERYONE COMES UP WITH GREAT IDEAS TO IMPROVE PERFORMANCE AND ADD VALUE. THEY INNOVATE IN EVERY ASPECT OF BUSINESS. THEY ARE RELENTLESS DISCOVERERS. THEY EXPLOIT TECHNOLOGY AND PLATFORMS.

5 THEY MANAGE AMBIGUITY AND KILL RISK:
THEY ARE COMFORTABLE WITH PARADOXES, MAKE THE COMPLEX SIMPLE, UNDERSTAND THE NEED FOR EVOLVING PLANS, THEY ARE AGILE. THEY ARE MENTALLY TOUGH AND RESILIENT TO DEAL WITH A WORLD IN PERPETUAL CRISIS. THEY ANTICIPATE AND KILL RISK QUICKLY. THEY STAY IN TOUCH WITH THE WORLD.

3 THEY CREATE HIGH PERFORMANCE TEAMS:
THEY ARE COMFORTABLE WITH COLLABORATION, EMPOWERMENT, AUTONOMY AND KNOW HOW TO BUILD TEAMS QUICKLY.

7 THEY DELIVER WITH PACE:
THEY TRANSLATE STRATEGY INTO MEANING AND INSPIRE ACTION, THEY JOIN THE DOTS, THEY ARE COMFORTABLE SPEEDING UP BY SLOWING DOWN, THEY DELIVER THROUGH PEOPLE AND TEAMS, THEY EXECUTE.

6 THEY EDUCATE:
THEY HELP PEOPLE AND ORGANISATIONS LEARN, THEY INSPIRE CURIOSITY, THEY ONLY TELL WHEN DIRECTION IS ABSOLUTELY NEEDED, THEY ENSURE LEARNING IS APPLIED, THEY LEAD WITH QUESTIONS, THEY COACH. THEY DEVELOP AND NURTURE CAPABILITY.

I AM UNSTOPPABLE

"NEVER, NEVER, NEVER GIVE UP"
WINSTON CHURCHILL